The Wisdom of Not-Knowing

essays on psychotherapy, Buddhism and life experience

edited by

Bob Chisholm and Jeff Harrison

Published in this first edition in 2016 by:

Triarchy Press

Axminster, England

+44 (0)1297 631456

info@triarchypress.net

www.triarchypress.net

A catalogue record for this book is available from the British Library.

Paperback ISBN: 978-1-909470-91-0

ePub ISBN: 978-1-909470-92-7

pdf ISBN: 978-1-909470-93-4

To go in the dark with a light is to know the light.
To know the dark, go dark. Go without sight,
and find that the dark, too, blooms and sings,
and is traveled by dark feet and dark wings.

Wendell Berry

Contents

Introduction

"All I know is that I know nothing."

Socrates

A collection of essays that is devoted to not-knowing might seem to have limited appeal. If knowledge represents power and makes any exercise of power possible, not-knowing might seem to amount to little more than a confession of ignorance and helplessness and would scarcely seem worthy of discussion. Yet as psychotherapists with backgrounds in Buddhism and existential phenomenology, we often find that the state of not-knowing can be a precursor to moments of rich discovery which possess a dynamic, transformative power that exceeds any prior expectation. Psychotherapy has always been aware that suspending judgement is often essential for therapy to be effective. The psychoanalyst Theodor Reik referred to this as "listening with the third ear", which is an attitude that allows for hidden and unexpected associations to rise to the therapist's conscious awareness by abstaining from automatic interpretation. Such listening requires heightened attentiveness by the therapist, yet by definition it cannot be clear quite what he or she will be attentive to. Even so, the sense of dynamic wonder which can animate the sense of not-knowing can often bring about the greatest changes in the course of therapy, particularly if the client can learn to cultivate a sense of not-knowing, too. Carl Jung, whose influence can be found in many of the articles presented in this volume, claimed that in his experience every successful course of psychotherapy hinged on an event that could not have been predicted beforehand. Our experience, which accords well with Jung's, prompted us to wonder further: could the experience of not-knowing be just as rich in hidden potential in other fields of endeavour?

The essays collected here offer abundant evidence that not-knowing does indeed figure importantly in many areas of life, so much so that we would go further: not-knowing is fundamental to conscious reflection and the desire to know must always arise in the first instance from the self-awareness of not-knowing. What the essays here offer is the testimony of people whose keen sense of not-knowing became the vital urge in their search for and discovery of meaning. While this book presents a wide range of approaches to not-knowing from the deeply personal, even confessional, to the more speculative and theoretical, behind each essay there is an impetus of deep wonder, which is the most essential feature in the dynamic of not-knowing. Perhaps we might even have referred to wonder in the title of this book. But in naming this collection, we took guidance from a remark by Noam Chomsky on the difference between problems and mysteries. Problems are matters that in principle, at least, are available for solutions. But mysteries are things that must lie beyond rational understanding. A good example of a problem in Chomsky's sense is how to bridge the gap between quantum physics and classical physics. This is, to be sure, a formidable problem to solve, but most physicists believe it will be solved in time by scientific methods. A good example of a mystery is existence itself. That we exist is not a mystery, it is a fact; but why we exist cannot be answered by any rational investigation of any amount of factual evidence and is thus a mystery. Wonder plays a vital role in addressing both problems and mysteries and we would be the first to admire the wonder that impels science to make its truly wondrous discoveries. But in this book we are concerned with mysteries rather than problems and unlike the wonder that drives science, the wonder with which this book is concerned can never result in hard, factual conclusions.

'Then why bother with such things?', many might wonder. Daniel Dennett, the philosopher and resolute materialist, for example, would certainly dismiss the reflections offered here as mere 'deepities' dispensed by what he calls mysterians. A deepity Dennett defines as "a proposition that seems to be profound because it is actually logically ill-formed. It has (at least) two meanings and balances precariously between them. On one reading it is true but trivial. And on another reading it is false, but would be earth-shattering if true." The vapid expression "love is just a word", is often cited as an example of a deepity. But Dennett also ridicules the theologian and former Archbishop of Canterbury Rowan Williams's description of faith as "silent waiting on the truth" as a mere deepity. We admire the robust way with which Dennett scorns hollow pseudo-profundities, but we confess that even as non-Christians we are in sympathy with Archbishop Williams. Although silent waiting on the truth can never stand as a principle of scientific verification, it expresses beautifully the suspended judgement and the quietening of the mind that are necessary for many authentic spiritual experiences. Moreover, in Dennett's views we find a certain hostility that rejects as fraudulent or deluded anything that can't be shown to be based in hard, scientific fact. We believe such brutal positivism will always remain deaf to the call of spirit and blind to the possibilities of not-knowing.

As we began to invite contributors to this book, we knew the theme of not-knowing would leave the door wide open to virtually anything. Our main interest was to find writers who knew from their own experiences and insights how rich in potential not-knowing can be. Psychotherapy does figure most prominently in this collection; but these essays have little technical or instructional content and speak for the most part from the personal experiences of the psychotherapist writers. What we found in their writing is what we ourselves find in our own therapeutic practices – not-knowing features far more often and far more importantly than most theory would suggest. Buddhism is also a strong influence in this collection as one contributor is a Buddhist monk and two others are former Buddhist monks. Moreover, many of the rest of us are lay Buddhists and are dedicated practitioners of Buddhist meditation. This is not, however, a book that promotes or purports to be about Buddhism, for it takes a much more inclusive approach to not-knowing. Indeed, if we had wanted, we could have drawn from a number of different spiritual traditions – Buddhist, Hindu, Christian, Jewish and Moslem – to demonstrate how intrinsic not-knowing is to spiritual and mystical experience in general. But nor is this a book about not-knowing as a prelude to mystical insight. It is about not-knowing as the experiential ground from which dynamic wonder arises. Thus, in the articles that deal respectively with herbalism, initiation into the therapeutic use of ayahuasca and a chance encounter in a Norwegian village, we see not-knowing as the vital element at work in various, yet always mysterious, processes of discovery.

As many articles draw on the work experiences of psychotherapists, not-knowing must be a consideration in our presentation, as well as the main thematic interest of our book. Perhaps no other relationship demands the confidentiality that psychotherapy requires, so we have made sure that the identities of all the clients discussed here have been safely concealed. Details of clients have been changed so comprehensively that only the author may know who he or she is actually discussing.

When we began this project we could not know in advance what the final result would be. But as we began to work closely with our collaborators we became increasingly confident that the book would meet the hopes we had placed in everyone's efforts. We have organised the essays so that various theoretical ideas about the nature of not-knowing precede testimonials of how not-knowing figured in a writer's personal experience. The contrast can be seen most sharply in the essays of Jeff Harrison and Ian Finlay. Harrison opts for a cool, analytical approach, whereas Finlay's highly personal reflections resemble an act of spiritual contemplation. Rosemary Lodge, Margaret Meyer and Owen Oakie all favour theoretical reflections over the more personal. But Manu Bazzano, Caroline Brazier, Alex Buchan, Bob Chisholm and Andy Paice draw deeply from their personal experiences to illustrate their more abstract ideas about not-knowing. Like Finlay, Paul Christelis and Jason Ranek have written autobiographical essays that largely dispense with extensive theorising and focus on the truth of their remarkable personal experiences. Structuring the book so that there is a progressive movement away from abstract ideas towards personal experience seemed to make sense to us as editors. But there is no need for the reader to approach the collection in such a consecutive fashion, as each essay is entirely capable of standing on its own. Even so, we believe that together these essays bring a breadth of insight to the experience of not-knowing that no single essay could do by itself.

We want to thank everyone who made this book possible, beginning with Caroline Brazier of the Tariki Trust who, before she contributed her fine essay to this collection, encouraged us to undertake this project in the first place. Indeed, Tariki can be regarded as the birthplace of this book and much of its content has its origins in the many spirited discussions that were held in Narborough. We want to thank all the other contributors to this volume, as well. A great deal of passion and effort went into each essay and each essay, in its own way, illuminates the ground of wonder that not-knowing can be. After reading this collection, we hope you will agree that not-knowing is something worth knowing about.

Bob Chisholm and Jeff Harrison

October 2015

Thresholds, Play, and Other Dangerous Things: Liminality and the Therapeutic Encounter

Margaret Meyer

How far into the depths must I reach in order to grasp that which seems at hand?

John Keats

The concept of liminality has its origin in the Latin word *limen*, 'threshold', a metaphor borrowed by the ethnographer Arnold van Gennep, and subsequently given wider currency by symbolic anthropologist Victor Turner. Studying and living with tribal cultures, both men became fascinated by the condition of liminality, the middle phase of a rite of passage, in which 'threshold' people – those undergoing a transition – symbolically 'die' to their former selves and are 'reborn' into a new state (Turner, 1969: 95).

> Liminality is conceived of as a season of silent, secret growth, a mediatory movement between what was and what will be, where the social process goes inward and underground for a time that is not profane time. (ibid: 279)

In observing the rituals and symbolism of transitional experiences, such as birth, adolescence, marriage and death, van Gennep identified a threefold structure, which he described as "separation, margin (or *limen*), and reincorporation", for which he also used the terms 'preliminal', 'liminal' and 'postliminal'. In the first phase, and in a move signifying the "death of the former self" and the start of a "sacred journey into what is not yet known", the threshold person ('liminar') may be physically detached from their community and relocated to a space, literally (and symbolically) on the margin of their daily life. Next, the transitioning person crosses a metaphoric threshold into a hybrid place, a space-time of paradox and ambiguity, "a ritual world removed from everyday notions of time and space" (Abrahams, in Turner, 1969: ix). In this domain, personal, psychological and societal norms can be questioned and challenged; the transitioning person "passes through a cultural realm that has few or none of the attributes of the past or coming state" (ibid: 94). The third and final phase marks the symbolic and literal return of the transitioning person, "inwardly transformed and outwardly changed", to a new place or role within the community (Turner, 1992: 48-9).

Van Gennep observed that the movement from the known world into the unknown is often prefaced by, or expressed as, "an opening of doors". These symbolic doors and gateways, and their accompanying physical or metaphysical structures (beams, lintels and thresholds) are among the most numinous symbols of crisis and transition. There may be doors and thresholds marking the different stages of the 'sacred journey', not only in time but in symbolic space: "The door is the boundary between the foreign and domestic worlds in the case of an ordinary dwelling, between the profane and sacred worlds in a temple. Therefore to cross the threshold is to unite oneself with a new world" (van Gennep, 1960: 20).

For Turner, this central liminal phase was most critical. In Turner's taxonomy, a *limen* denotes a symbolically charged space-time, sometimes very protracted – a corridor or "a tunnel which may become a pilgrim's road" (1992: 49). To cross the threshold into liminality is to enter into experiences characterised by uncertainty, ambiguity and disruption. In this space between 'ordered worlds', at once disturbing and richly creative, a threshold person may, for a time at least, free themselves of psycho-social requirements, expectations and scripts. The symbolic passage is a journey, and the liminal 'traveller' both no man and everyman, being "not this or that, here or there, one thing or the other" – a natural consequence of being "betwixt and between" the known categories of ordinary social and psychological life (1974: 53). Liminality, wrote Turner, is a realm "'where there is a certain freedom to juggle with the factors of existence" (1967:106). Paradox and polarity are among the most distinctive characteristics of the liminal state, which is likened to "death, to being in the womb, to invisibility, to darkness, to bisexuality, to the wilderness, and to an eclipse of the sun or moon" (1969: 95). Transitioning people may act out or embody a radical ambiguity, being neither an old self nor (yet) the new. In this state, things that seem fixed, given and known, both in the outward world and within the psyche, can be appraised, critiqued and possibly reordered. In consequence, the threat to personal identity is profound; that which can be reordered can become, for a time at least, unrecognisable. Clearly, such challenge is not without risk. In the tribal cultures studied by van Gennep and Turner, this risk is mitigated, if not removed, with the aid of ritual process and symbols designed to compensate for this most profound challenge to identity. Turner especially understood the psycho-spiritual significance of liminal processes, finding in them a commonwealth of metaphors capable of addressing the most fundamental human polarities: order and disorder, making and unmaking, knowing and not-knowing.

> Undoing, dissolution, decomposition are accompanied by processes of growth, transformation, and the reformulation of old elements in new patterns. [...] This coincidence of opposite processes and notions in a single representation characterizes the peculiar unity of the liminal: that which is neither this nor that, and yet is both. (Turner, 1967: 99)

An anthropologist, Turner's focus was on social structures. Correspondingly, his work placed less emphasis on the personal implications of liminality. With due deference, and in offering a re-reading of the liminal paradigm through a psychotherapeutic lens, I am proposing that that it offers tremendous potential for both therapist and client. Of course, in so doing I am taking certain liberties with the liminal paradigm. But in recasting it so as to foreground its psychological potential I do not believe that I am reducing its potency. Rather, I suggest that the metaphors of liminality, if not its whole schema (of separation, transition and integration), offer both client and therapist a framework for negotiating the fact of not-knowing. Certainly in my own practice it is a framework I turn to during moments when I or my clients are experiencing not-knowing, or struggling to grasp something that is only partially known, or a knowing that oscillates between the foreground and background of our awareness.

The simple act of taking the 'known knowns' of a client's *modus vivendi* and subjecting them to question and reordering is in itself a threshold act. Conversely, it seems to me, thresholds are likely to present themselves at junctures in life when there is a need for reappraisal; they may be invoked or invited, but more often they are occasioned by the psychological crises that accompany major life events (birth, adolescence, marriage, death). As discussed elsewhere in this volume, people come into therapy for a multiplicity of reasons. The need for support in negotiating the 'unknown unknowns' of a threshold is one. In fact the practice of psychotherapy is a response to the problem of not-knowing – a problem much less admissible in industrialised cultures in which our dominant metaphors are of conquest and control. Amongst other tasks, the project of therapy is to offer assistance to a threshold person on a journey into liminality; company and containment in exploring what is not known; and to enable a client to make the most (if they choose) of thresholds, literal and metaphoric.

This is especially evident at the start of therapy, when a new client is in effect contracting to separate, at least for the duration of a therapeutic hour, from established ('sedimented', to borrow Merleau-Ponty's apposite phrase) patterns of being and thinking. Most therapists have observed the way new clients may linger on the physical threshold of a practice room, sometimes needing more than one invitation to enter the space, or to leave it. In this most liminal of places, poised or paused between the therapeutic space and everyday life, a client may make important disclosures, experience an insight, or acknowledge a previously inadmissible truth.

Gordon, who came into therapy after his wife had given him "an ultimatum", threatening to end their 30-year marriage, lingered each week in the doorway, reluctant to enter and subsequently reluctant to leave. Such pauses were in marked contrast to almost every other aspect of Gordon's behaviour. Once through the doorway, Gordon spoke, walked and gestured very quickly; speed was habitual to him. Aged 54, he had enjoyed a stellar career in banking which was about to come to an abrupt and totally unexpected end: he was being made redundant. For Gordon this news was simply "catastrophic". Already a heavy drinker and smoker, he reacted to this "body blow" by upping his consumption of both and being verbally abusive to his wife. The abuse culminated in a volcanic row in the small hours of one morning. After this incident his wife had given him notice "to get myself together, or go". Reluctantly, Gordon had agreed to seek help. But his not knowing, week to week, whether he would be able to afford to continue with therapy, or whether he even wanted to continue, were simultaneously a response to a wider uncertainty, and a stratagem for keeping both of us in a state of not-knowing.

In presenting the partial retelling of Gordon's story that follows, I have greatly abridged it so as to make its liminal aspects more obvious. To my surprise, and I think to Gordon's also, he did continue with therapy. In the months that followed I began to understand how difficult it was for him to put into words what was really important: his old grammars of expression, which related to his identity as a successful professional man, had been stripped away with the redundancy notice. And although Gordon talked a great deal, packing great quantities of words into long sentences, a feature of his monologues was that, for all the verbiage, it was difficult to locate the 'meat' of his communication. Pressing him to articulate what he thought or felt in the moment could be a stressful experience for both of us. In this transitional period Gordon was literally at a loss, no longer his former self and yet to arrive at a new self-construct with the vocabulary that he supposed might go with it.

Turner describes in some detail and with great insight the intensity of this transition or 'mid-liminal' period, during which the symbolic journey is "essentially unstructured". At the same time this lack of the conventional, the known knowns, can also present opportunities to experiment, make discoveries, and to play:

> Liminality is particularly conducive to play. Play is not to be restricted to games and jokes; it extends to the introduction of new forms of symbolic action, such as word games or masks. In short, parts of liminality may be given over to experimental behaviour. Here I mean by 'experiment' any action or process undertaken to discover something not yet known [...] In liminality, new ways of acting, new combinations of symbols, are tried out, to be discarded or accepted. (Turner, 1992: 52)

Most therapists will be comfortable with the concept of 'experimental behaviour', for that is what Gordon was engaged in. Perhaps less obvious is how 'play' and 'symbolic action' translate into therapy. In my practice, play is made possible through metaphor and symbol, the *lingua franca* of both native human experience and (according to Turner) liminality. We think in metaphor and so we express ourselves in it: an astonishing six to eight metaphors per minute to communicate quite ordinary things. We have a particular need for metaphor when we are trying to express feelings, emotions and values, or very abstract concepts such as our experience of time and space. At these times we reach for metaphors that are mostly drawn from our felt sense of inhabiting bodies in a physical world. For example, in the context of a therapeutic conversation, metaphors bring with them important jumping-off points for exploring psychological (and physical) processes, unpacking difficult emotions and experiences, or rehearsing possibilities that everyday logic might otherwise close down. Above all, a client's metaphors provide us with a very natural way of shifting attention: from what is in the foreground of their awareness to the background themes, patterns and intuitions that may be intuitively sensed but not consciously acknowledged.

In Gordon's case, working more directly with a literal threshold allowed him to investigate, name and live more comfortably with the truth of his liminal life-stage. Over some weeks, the space just inside the door of my practice room began to take on special significance. Gordon continued to pause there, sometimes for many minutes, both on the way in and on the way out. Clients do not always like these thresholds of not-knowing; they struggle to put into words what it is they do not know, or would like to know; and, having done so, they may not like their own expressions. Yet, here Gordon would stand without speaking, unusual for one so talkative. In retrospect I believe our mutual and intuitive recognition of the potency of this space allowed Gordon to speak for the aspects of his experience and self-narrative that he found difficult to express. Little by little he found that he could speak to the threshold, or conversely the threshold might speak to or for him. Eventually, in one charged and very memorable session, he was able to experiment, using my practice room as a proxy, with the prospect of 'separating' from his employment, and possibly also from his marriage. He did this by opening the door, traversing the threshold in a kind of slow motion during which I encouraged him to report his experience at almost every step, and then stepping into a new, hybrid state in which he was a retired, separated, but not-yet divorced man.

*

A challenge inherent in the process of coming to terms with, or working through, not-knowing, is that it can only proceed at its own pace. There cannot be – as Keats so aptly expressed – "an irritable reaching after fact", because the 'facts', as the client originally perceived them, have a tendency to shift, "like quicksand", as Gordon told me. And indeed they did. Having negotiated one threshold, the emphasis of our work turned to another. Presenting for his seventeenth session, Gordon made an important admission: that his chronic insomnia was "part and parcel" and a definite contributor to the problems in his marriage. Certainly, the dark rings under his eyes provided visual proof of his struggle for sleep. As the session unfolded, Gordon talked about being sent to boarding school aged 12 by parents concerned that their bright, insatiably curious young son should have the best possible education. As he struggled to put into words the memory of this experience, he could for the first time acknowledge his distress at being sent away from his family. Unsurprisingly, his sleeplessness had started at this time and persisted into adulthood. What Gordon had come to appreciate was that the pairing of "desperate busyness" followed by the exhaustion arising from so little sleep had become firmly woven into his way of being-in-the-world and – more importantly – of being-in-his-marriage. His fatigue directly undermined Gordon's ability to be present to his wife and children, or to take part as fully as he might in family life. Moreover, he added, with the tonalities of shame coming into his voice, he could now admit that his irritability and legendary short temper, both natural consequences of lack of sleep, but which Gordon had justified and even incorporated into his professional persona, had probably played a leading role in eliciting his redundancy notices from his career and his marriage. If he were able to sleep for a full night, waking at a 'sensible time' (the same time as his wife), Gordon thought that he could become more present to the marriage and more attuned to his wife.

Amongst other things, sleep is an opportunity for the conscious (waking) mind to rest, replenish itself – and to not-know. Many of the metaphors we have for sleep confirm this: to sink into darkness, into a void, into oblivion, into stillness. For Gordon, sleep was a great paradox: he craved it, and yet he also feared it. Sleep represented "a great blank": everything that was uncertain, beyond Gordon's control, and unknown. In consequence, Gordon's evenings were filled with anxiety: he did not want to surrender to "the blank", but he did want relief from "this anxiety, that follows me everywhere, like a stalker". From the moment he woke (typically, sometime between 3 and 4am) until he went to bed at around midnight, Gordon was, he told me, "aggressively awake". By this he meant that he read prolifically; he had kept all his subscriptions to professional journals, and his evenings were spent consuming them (together with many bottles of wine) and interrogating the web. Yet in the very next sentence, he proclaimed that he could sleep anywhere, listing numerous occasions when he had done just that. "I have even", he said proudly, "slept for three hours at Birmingham station – during the rush hour!" Playing back to him what I had just heard, I pointed out what was seemingly obvious: that, in fact, Gordon had the ability to sleep almost anywhere, at almost any time.

This was a cue for Gordon's eyelids to drop closed like curtains coming down on a stage; his head fell back, his breathing deepened, and he fell quite spontaneously into something that looked very much like sleep. All my queries to discover what had happened, and to check that Gordon was all right, were met with silence. Drawing on my training (in Ericksonian hypno-psychotherapy), I surmised that he had put himself into a state of trance. Lapsing into silence myself, I sat contemplating this new development.

Here I must qualify what I mean by 'trance' because the perception of it has become so gothic. The state of trance is a naturally occurring phenomenon: we are cycling in and out of these states (which may last moments or many minutes) at regular intervals in a 24-hour period. Anyone who has emerged from a daydream, driven from one place to another as if on auto-pilot ('highway hypnosis'), or fallen into a reverie whilst listening to music or watching television ('TV trance') has had an experience of the trance state.

To my mind, trance is a category of experience that is firmly liminal. Lying somewhere between sleep and everyday consciousness, it is a threshold state of 'radical ambiguity' (to employ Turner's phrase). Whether invited by the therapist or generated by the client, trance is very much an instance of the 'gap between ordered worlds' that caught Turner's attention; a gap in which to 'quiet' cognitive function so as to allow subliminal content (literally, that which is below the threshold of awareness) to come to the fore. It has tremendous value in healing because it enables a client to reflect on and, if necessary, reorder their inner meaning-world. In therapeutic trance, a client may review and rework limiting self-constructs and imagine more positive alternatives. Someone who has experienced trauma may, for example, discover how to 'unknow' the experience by enlisting the help of the subconscious to blur traumatic details, or shift the whole memory from a horribly consuming centre-stage into the wings of their awareness. A client suffering from chronic pain can identify times in life, and places in the body, where there has been, or is, no pain; then use these new 'knowns' to construct further experiences of not-knowing pain. In short, therapeutic trance provides an opportunity to work with the bedrock of a client's self-construct, offering the freedom, should the client choose to take it, to play with the knowns and unknowns of their self-narrative.

However, the demands on the therapist are considerable, not least because of the need to stay open to client experiences, the intensity and meaning of which can be totally unknown. For me, it provides proof positive of the truth of Keats's concept of 'negative capability', when both therapist and client are "capable of being in uncertainties, mysteries, doubts, without any irritable reaching after fact or reason" (Keats, 1899: 277).

This was certainly my experience at this moment. While it seemed clear that my comment had precipitated Gordon's hypnotic reverie, I did not know, and could not know, exactly what was occurring. I could not know the nature of Gordon's mental process in these moments, or even more practical details, such as for how long his trance would last. I could only work with two things: the observable 'data' of Gordon's trance, such as the evenness of his breathing (a relief, and a positive indication that all was well) and my own process: one of holding myself in something of a threshold state, of positive not-knowing.

It is possible to view the unfolding of therapy as an extended rite of passage, containing many liminal episodes (within many therapeutic encounters) in which established modes of behaviour may be suspended and challenged. The client brings content from his or her unique meaning-world (perceptions, assumptions, memories, beliefs, phantasies and values): the therapeutic encounter exists, at the very least, to provide opportunities for exploration. The client's project may be to 'know' or 'understand' such content, but there is no guarantee that knowing will be possible. It is in these sessions, when the work seems to have reached a crux of not-knowing, that I reach for the liminal paradigm. I find it *helpful* both as a theoretical construct and as a lived structure in which I can place and hold my own not-knowing. Using the model in this way helps me contain my concerns, for example, that the therapy seems to have lost its way; or to manage my own frustration when the work has become repetitive or when the client persists in not-knowing something that seems perfectly clear, even obvious, to me. These concerns arise from my own frame of reference, and I find it a good discipline to remind myself of the necessity of striking a balance between the client's welfare (particularly while s/he is in trance), and staying open to the emergent possibilities of the therapeutic conversation. Ernesto Spinelli, writing as an existential practitioner, has coined the term 'un-knowing' to describe the challenge, for therapists, in treating "the seemingly familiar [...] as novel, unfixed in meaning, accessible to previously unexamined possibilities" (1997: 6).

Eventually, after about 25 minutes, Gordon surfaced into ordinary consciousness. He was only partially aware that he had been in trance, and he could not remember anything of his experience except to say that he felt very relaxed. We reflected on the fact that he had managed to fall into a sleep of sorts (hypnosis comes from the Greek *hypnos*, meaning 'sleep'), simply by focusing on his ability to do just that. Our hour was up and Gordon prepared to leave. As was usual for him, he paused at the door and wondered out loud whether it was possible that there could be a "magic bullet" for the problem of his insomnia.

Time did not allow us any further exploration of that idea. But the following week Gordon arrived for his session carrying a bullet casing strung on a length of garden twine. With pride, he told me that he had managed to sleep for a whole week from midnight to 7am. He could not account for this dramatic change; something – he couldn't think what – had occurred to prompt it. Intuitively, he had translated this new knowing into symbolic form. True enough, he had woken at his usual time of 3am, but had been able to get to sleep again by using the magic bullet as a pendulum. "There's something about its swaying…" he muttered, dangling the bullet so that it began to rock and swing. Within moments and still on his feet, he was asleep.

Gordon's story ended as it began, on a threshold of not (quite) knowing, sandwiched between the difficult 'facts' of old and emerging life narratives. In due course, about two-thirds of the way into the year, Gordon announced that he had decided to discontinue therapy. Using part of his redundancy payout, he was going to Indonesia to stay with his brother-in-law, who had just opened a hotel there. In this place, away from home but not quite separated from his family, he could think, reappraise – and sleep. Even now, years later, I remain indebted to him, for all that he taught me about the potential of liminality.

References

Keats, J. (1899) *The Complete Poetical Works and Letters of John Keats*, Cambridge Edition, Houghton, Mifflin

Lakoff, G. & Johnson, M. (1980/2003) *Metaphors We Live By*, University of Chicago Press

Spinelli, E. (1997) *Tales of Un-Knowing: Therapeutic Encounters from an Existential Perspective*, PCCS Books

Turner, V. (1967) *The Forest of Symbols: Aspects of Ndembu Ritual*, Cornell University Press

____ (1969) *The Ritual Process: Structure and Anti-Structure*, Aldine Transactions

____ (1992) *Blazing the Trail: Way Marks in the Exploration of Symbols*, University of Arizona Press

van Gennep, A. (1960) *The Rites of Passage*, University of Chicago Press

Sometimes We Don't Know What We Know: The Importance of Emotional or Hidden Knowledge

Rosemary Lodge

Introduction

Before thinking about the concept of not-knowing we probably need to go back a few steps and first ask *what* knowing actually is and *how* we know things. In the West we tend to assume that we can only know things if we can see them or work them out logically and conceptually. We favour the kind of knowledge that can be written down, calculated, easily communicated from one person to another; the type of knowledge that is rational, logical, conceptual and most of all provable. All these types of knowledge might best be described as being located in the cognitive mind – and as forming part of consciousness. We are aware of this knowledge – we know what we know. The situation might change over time as more and more knowledge proves that earlier knowledge was not quite accurate, but essentially it feels as if this kind of knowledge can somehow be tested or proved and that it has some direct correspondence with 'reality' or the 'truth', against which we can test it. Apart from in certain areas of quantum physics, this kind of knowledge often rests on an assumption that truth or reality is fixed and secure to a large degree.

However, cognitive knowledge is not the only kind of knowledge. The existential philosophers such as Kierkegaard and Sartre argued for a different type of knowledge – for a more subjective, experiential knowledge. This is knowledge that cannot be proved and which is unique to each person. An important part of experiential subjective knowledge is *emotional* knowing and this is the focus of this essay. In any situation I not only cognitively appraise what is happening, I also have an emotional, 'felt sense' response to it. Emotions have a complex relationship with cognitions, but there is some evidence that not all emotional knowing passes through our conscious cognitive mind. This might suggest that consciousness is not solely located in the mind, in our cognitive processes, but also resides in the body and in our emotional knowing. If we argue that knowing something cognitively locates it in the mind (I am aware of it therefore I know it) might we locate a different type of knowing (which might appear to be 'not-knowing' because we are not cognitively or consciously aware of it) in the body and in our emotional responses to things?

This essay will argue that this different type of knowing might initially be conceptualised as not-knowing simply because it is the space in which certain types of knowledge reside before, possibly, entering conscious, cognitive knowing. However, it is also a potential source of wisdom and useful knowledge that, if attended to, can lead to growth and change. I will draw on my own research into the experience of emotional connection in therapy which has shown that emotional knowledge, particularly subliminal emotional knowledge, plays a key role in client change.

'Emotions' and 'Feelings'

If we are going to talk about emotional knowledge we should probably start with trying to define exactly what we mean when we talk about an emotion. There is no agreed answer as to what an emotion or a feeling actually is. Scientists, philosophers and psychologists have attempted to define emotions, without ever coming to a definitive or consensual understanding. Emotions have been studied as biological functions of the nervous system or as psychological states independent of brain mechanisms (Damasio, 2000). They have been seen as primitive, base responses to be mastered by reason or as an essential guide to our being in the world (van Deurzen, 2002).

However, there is one area in which there does seem to be some agreement – which is that emotions have a complex relationship with cognitions. One way to approach emotions, therefore, may be to try to unpick this relationship – how do cognitions and emotions interact with each other, and is it possible to have emotions without cognitions and vice versa? This directly relates to the question of different types of knowledge and how they may interact. There does seem to be evidence that not all emotional experiences are the same: some may have *less* cognitive content (being unconscious or unreflected on) whereas others may have *more* cognitive content (being either reflected on or including personal and social meanings). Carl Rogers, the humanistic psychologist, made the following distinction between emotions and feelings: he suggested that an emotion was a physical sensation or reaction to the environment whereas a feeling was the product of the *symbolisation* of experience. A feeling would therefore also include the *cognitive* meanings of experience:

> A feeling denotes an emotionally tinged experience, together with its personal meaning. Thus it includes the emotion in its experiential context. It thus refers to the unity of emotion and cognition as they are experienced inseparably in the moment. (Rogers, cited in Greenberg et al, 1993)

Rogers's definition seems to imply that it may be possible to have an emotional experience (an unreflective, automatic response to the environment) without any cognitive element to it and vice versa – and that feelings are a kind of unifying bridge between them.

The difference can be illustrated by thinking about anger. Let's suppose a young child has their favourite toy stolen by another child at school. The straightforward emotional response is one of anger at this boundary violation, directed at the offending child: an un-thought-about response. However, when the child returns home to tell her mum about what happened, let's suppose the mother, rather than reflecting back this emotional response and supporting her daughter, starts to blame the daughter for what happened: "You should never have taken that toy into school, I told you not to, you can't trust anyone, I told you this would happen." Perhaps when the daughter recounts how she shouted at the offending child, the mother also starts lecturing the child on 'inappropriate behaviour' – telling her "never shout at another child" and "girls shouldn't get angry", etc. The mother, tied up in her own emotional responses of shame and blame, cannot empathise with her daughter. The daughter now has a much more complicated web of meanings surrounding anger – some particular to her own family's responses, and some from wider societal responses. Anger is no longer a straightforward response to a violation, it is now something that can be reflected upon and which has various meanings attached to it. Let's fast forward to adulthood. Now, when someone crosses the woman's boundaries, instead of having a straightforward emotional response of anger, she may experience a whole range of feelings – all connected to and embedded in a complex pattern of meanings. Perhaps she experiences an initial shaft of anger, followed quickly by the feeling that she should bite her tongue, followed quickly again by searching for whether she is somehow to blame for the boundary violation, then by the feeling that she has somehow behaved in an unfeminine manner, all accompanied by a sense of shame and low self-worth. Anger is no longer a clean emotional response triggered by the environment – it has become a complex web of feelings (emotions and cognitions) that are connected to how she now experiences 'anger'.

Rogers was not alone in making such a distinction: other theorists also distinguish (though in different ways) those emotions that have a cognitive element from those that do not. For example, Greenberg (2003) suggests that an affect is an *unconscious* biological response to stimulation, involving automatic neural processes connected with the evolutionary adaptive behavioural response system; a feeling involves awareness of the basic sensations of affect (either at a simple level, e.g. feeling shaky, or at a more complex level, involving felt meaning); and emotions are experiences that arise when action tendencies and feeling states are joined with evoking situations and the self. As such, an emotion involves the integration of many levels of processing and gives personal meaning to our experience.

Denzin (1984) draws a distinction between emotional unconsciousness and emotional consciousness suggesting that, in the former, it is possible to experience emotions in an unreflective state as contrasted with the latter which is a more reflective state, and in which a person is able to guide, direct, or interpret emotion as he or she is feeling it. Similarly, Strasser (1999) distinguishes between reflective and unreflective emotions – using the term which he derives from Sartre. Damasio (2000), a neuroscientist who has researched brain function extensively, also maintains that there is evidence to suggest that we are not conscious of all our feelings.

Emotions and cognitions may be separate processes

It seems then that, although there is much debate about what an emotion or a feeling actually is, there is some support for the idea that an emotion may be unconscious or pre-reflective, or may be more complex, involving cognitions and personal meanings. The implication of this may be that emotions and cognitions are separate, but intertwined, processes. Greenberg (1997) specifically suggests that a person has *separate* emotional and cognitive systems, and that the emotional system may operate at a pre-conscious level. He believes that a person processes information in two different ways – experientially and conceptually. Conceptual processing is about causal reasoning, logic, analytical thinking and the development of narrative explanations, whereas experiential processing is concerned with the implicit emotional meanings in things as related to our own well-being. Conceptual processing can provide a kind of abstract, intellectual knowing about oneself and a set of learned values or a set of rules of how one ought to be (like Rogers's conditions of worth), such values being developed from others' expectations and not from personal experience. By contrast, experiential processing is rooted in a person's own experience and is not a cognitive appraisal of whether something is true or false; rather, it is an *emotional* appraisal of whether something is safe or dangerous, enhancing or diminishing. We are probably all familiar with this distinction between how we think we ought to feel and how we actually do feel. How many times have you said to yourself something like 'I know I shouldn't get upset over such a trivial matter, it's just not important in the grand scheme of things, but I just can't seem to help myself'?

Langs (1995) also suggests that emotional and conceptual processing are separate processes. His communicative approach to psychotherapy is based on his theory about the architecture of the human mind. This theory arose from a phenomenon he noticed in therapy, namely that patients' narratives often seemed to be unconscious communications about the therapeutic 'here and now'. He proposed that the mind has a 'deep unconscious system' (DUS) designed to deal with *emotional* inputs, and that these inputs, especially if emotionally threatening, *would go straight to the DUS without passing through consciousness.* He theorised that there was an emotional processing part of the mind that was quite separate from the conscious, cognitive processing part. It is, therefore, a theory about unconscious or subliminal emotional processing.

How might this look in practice? Let's suppose a male therapist is late for an appointment with his client. The following time the pair meet the client starts talking about how his dad was always late picking him up from football practice and how distressing this experience was. The therapist is struck by the similarity of the story to the situation from the previous week and assumes that his own lateness has had an impact on the client of which the client is unaware. In other words, the therapist interprets the client's narrative as an unconscious communication about the therapist himself. The therapist's lateness has triggered an emotional response in the client that is threatening and which therefore bypasses his cognitive awareness and goes directly into the man's emotional brain. This emotional 'knowledge' can be brought into consciousness by the skill of the therapist by correctly spotting and interpreting it. In this example, the therapist might empathise with the client's felt sense of what it was like when his dad was late and possibly link it to the here and now situation of the therapist's own lateness.

The idea that we may not always be aware of how we feel about things is not new. Freud had suggested something similar when he talked about the unconscious – which he saw as being guarded by the 'censor' which would decide whether to send inputs to the unconscious (if emotionally threatening) or to consciousness. Sartre (2003) criticised Freud's idea on the basis that if the censor 'knew' everything in order to decide which way to send it then it actually did know what it didn't know and was therefore in bad faith. However, LeDoux's (1998) research has shown that all information comes into us via two quite distinct pathways – the emotional processing route (which is fast, and rough and ready) and the cognitive processing route (which is slightly slower but more considered and therefore more 'accurate') – and that one can therefore have an emotional experience that does not pass through the cognitive part of our brains so that we are not 'conscious' of it. This idea that information enters via two distinct pathways would provide an answer to Sartre's criticism – we may 'know' what is in the emotional processing part of our minds and bodies, but not in the traditional sense of knowing – we don't have conscious, cognitive awareness, although arguably it is available for us to turn our attention to.

There is a debate about whether such an emotional processing part of the mind could be truly called unconscious (see for example Spinelli (1993, 1994) who suggests that it is pre-reflective rather than unconscious). However, whether one talks about unconscious or pre-reflective emotional responses, there is are indications of an emotional processing part of the mind that, at least initially, operates separately from the cognitive part of the mind.

'Being' and 'Doing' may not be in harmony

One of the implications of emotional and cognitive processing systems being separate is that they may not always be working in harmony with each other – they may be incongruent. Rogers had a theory about incongruence and its importance in relation to mental health and therapeutic work. A basic definition of incongruence is: what a person says or how a person acts is not in accordance with how they feel. It is something that is hard to define, but we all know it when we see it. This is the person who might appear friendly and jovial but whose 'jokes' cut to the quick and make one feel small; the person who appears polite but who seems to evoke anger in those around them by their passivity or helplessness. These are people who don't act in accordance with how they feel – not in a socially adapted way of masking their emotions for the sake of harmonious relationships (politeness), but who seem oblivious to the emotional atmosphere that they give off.

The very notion of incongruence contains within it an implicit assumption that emotions may be more or less conscious: if one can act without awareness or in a way that is not congruent, then there must be some part of our 'being' or experience that is not consciously thought about, attended to or symbolised. Gendlin suggested that congruence only made sense if there was such a thing as *pre-conceptual* experience against which to check the congruity of words spoken or actions taken (1997). He proposed that pre-conceptual experience was something real and separate from (but available to) symbolisation and that, regardless of content or symbolisation, there is always a process of experience within a person:

> ...there always is the concretely present flow of feeling: at any moment we can individually and privately direct our attention inward, and when we do that, there it is [...] Whether we name it, divide it, or not, there it is. (Gendlin, 1997: 11)

Since both Rogers and Gendlin acknowledge that feelings involve some level of cognitive activity, I would suggest that the pre-conceptual experience against which one checks the accuracy/congruence of words/actions/feelings is, therefore, at its most fundamental level, an emotional level. It is, then, a question of checking whether my thoughts, words and actions are in harmony with a more pre-verbal, emotional self.

As a result, one of the implications of our having separate emotional and cognitive processing systems is that they may not always be working in harmony. We might try to override our emotional experience by imposing cognitive structures that simply don't fit. For example, my experience of a person may be that I feel unsafe when around them – but this is too threatening to acknowledge, or I may not trust my experience, or I may simply not pay attention to this kind of knowledge, so I tell myself that I am being silly and that this person is perfectly nice. I ignore my experiential emotional knowledge and give priority to my learned cognitive response which may come from family or societal rules – such as 'be polite to people', 'don't be too quick to judge', 'trust the doctor' and so on. Where a person's cognitive processing dominates or continually contradicts a person's emotional experience it can leave the person unable to function in an integrated manner. R.D. Laing described this state of affairs in *The Divided Self* (1990).

Greenberg (2003) also specifically suggests that it is possible for a person's emotional schema and intellectual processing to be incongruent or not working in harmony. He proposes that when a person's conceptual meanings dominate, contradict or override his or her emotional experience, that person will be unable to function optimally, unable to rely on their own basic orientation system and will become split, in the words of Laing, into "divided or false selves" (1990: 69).

It has been suggested that one of the reasons that the emotional and rational sides of a person may not operate in harmony with each other is that there is poor communication between the two systems. Langs (1995) suggested that communication between the DUS and consciousness is very poor. LeDoux (1998) found that connections between the emotional and the cognitive systems were weak, particularly in one direction: he found that it is easier for emotions to flood the cognitive mind than it is to use reason to try to gain control over our emotions.

Change happens at the feeling level

What are the implications for therapy of this possible disharmony between emotional and cognitive systems, and poor communication between them? Some models of therapy conceptualise the process as being one of trying to facilitate greater integration between the systems, but different approaches are used to achieve this. In cognitive therapy, the starting point is a person's thoughts or cognitive system. The emphasis is on changing the way that a person *thinks* because it is argued that emotions follow thoughts and that the kind of thoughts a person has will determine the kind of emotion they feel:

> The specific content of the interpretation of an event leads to a specific emotional response [...] depending on the kind of interpretation a person makes, he will feel glad, sad, scared, or angry – or he may have no particular emotional reaction at all. (Beck, 1976: 51-52)

Thoughts and emotions are seen as intricately and instrumentally linked, and attempts to change a person are made through the thinking route. The primary emphasis is on breaking out of negative chains of cognition, behaviour and emotion via the cognitive and behavioural ports of entry (Scott and Dryden, 2003). Change in this model is often synonymous with behaviour change. However, other approaches suggest that greater integration of thoughts and feelings is attained by starting with the *emotional* level as it is emotion that is the most influential part of the creation of personal meaning and emotional processing is more powerful than conceptual processing. Greenberg (1997) suggests that it is *emotion* that guides our lives, setting goals, regulating mental functioning and organising thought and action, and that cognition simply finds a way to meet the goals set by emotion. He proposes that it is not possible to change a person's emotional schema by working at the conceptual level: his clinical experience has shown that intellectual knowledge about the self does not effect deep or lasting change because such knowledge does not affect *emotion* structures, which are what govern behaviour.

Other therapeutic models have an understanding of this difficulty and implicitly suggest that the work of therapy must start at the emotional level. In these types of therapy the therapeutic process is conceptualised as one which involves putting feelings into words. Rogers suggested that the therapeutic process of change involves a recognition, and naming, of feelings so that the client moves away from a state in which feelings are unrecognised, un-owned and unexpressed towards a state in which 'ever changing feelings are experienced in the moment, knowingly and acceptingly, and may be accurately expressed' (1961: 64). The end point of the process for Rogers was that the client just *is* his or her experience and formulates himself or herself out of that experience, rather than trying to impose a formulation of the self onto experience. In other words it was a process of words flowing out of emotions rather than trying to impose words onto emotion. Gendlin (1996) also emphasised the importance of putting feelings into words and suggested that, where a client is able to accurately describe in words their own felt sense of themselves, this brings about a shift in a person without the need for explanation. Similarly, from an existential perspective, Strasser (1999) suggests that it is one of the aims of therapy to explore emotions but particularly to "facilitate the unreflective emotions to emerge into reflective ones" (p.27) so that they can be examined, discussed and challenged.

In the communicative approach, Langs (1995) suggested that therapy worked by accessing what was hidden in the client's emotional unconscious and correctly describing it, and he developed a therapeutic technique known as 'trigger decoding' in an attempt to do this. He found that, if the therapist finds the right word to correctly describe the client's underlying, currently lived feeling (that is, the feelings arising in response to the therapeutic 'here and now'), it 'has a profound impact on the basic unconscious cognitive schemata through which the patient organises his or her experiences of the world' (Smith, 1991: 217). This is similar to Gendlin and Rogers who both placed emphasis on the importance of finding the right word to describe the feeling.

LeDoux's (1998) research supports the idea that it is easier to effect change at the emotional level. As noted, he found that connections from the emotional system to the cognitive system were stronger than the other way round and so proposed that therapy should take place at the emotional, not verbal, level, it being simply too difficult to get conscious control over emotions.

Re-living emotional experiences

Some theorists also suggest that most change will happen if the client is able to actually experience emotional responses in the therapeutic 'here and now' – in other words that therapy is not just about finding the right words to describe past emotions or emotions experienced outside the therapy room but about actually experiencing deep affective responses with the therapist. Greenberg (2003), for example, specifically suggests that change can only take place if a client has a 'hot' emotional experience – that is, the client needs to *re-live in present awareness* an emotional experience of, say, unloveableness or inadequacy rather than access an intellectual concept of these emotions. The idea is that the therapist helps the client to relive emotional experiences and to symbolise them so that they become accessible for change.

This was certainly what I found in my own research into emotional connection in therapy. Having interviewed client-therapist pairs separately about their experience of the same therapy session, analysis of the data suggested that emotional experiences in therapy were more effective at helping clients heal than simply talking about emotional issues. All the clients drew a distinction between talking about issues and actually having an emotional experience of the issue in question. For example, one client had been working on trying to allow herself to get angry in order to be more assertive in her life. It wasn't until she actually had an experience of being angry in the therapy session itself that she was able to make real changes in this area. I also found, looking at all five therapeutic pairs, that the less conceptualising and interpreting the therapist did, and the more the therapist just allowed very strong emotions to surface, the deeper the level of change that seemed to be stirred in the client.

Greenberg draws a distinction between different emotions, suggesting that they have different functions (for example, anger warns us of danger, love moves us towards people) and that some emotions are primary emotions with clear adaptive value (sadness at loss, anger at violation) whilst others are secondary emotions that are more highly mediated and socially influenced. According to Greenberg, working with primary emotions in therapy involves simply expressing and allowing. This then evokes the relevant action tendency. For example, a client who is able to fully feel and express anger at childhood abuse will thereby access the related action tendency to push the offender away and establish boundaries. By contrast, work with secondary or instrumental emotions may include accessing a person's whole relationship with the emotion. However, in each case he suggests that the client must actually access the relevant emotion in the therapy room with the therapist in order to effect change.

In the psychodynamic therapies there has also been an interest in the patient's emotional experiences with the analyst. Maroda (1998) suggests that psychodynamic therapies have traditionally been seen to value intellectualisation over and above emotional experiences. However, she re-emphasises the primary importance of *emotional* experiences in therapy and suggests that these must come *first* - before interpretations. She has found, in her own clinical experience, that intellectual insights follow *emotional* shifts; and that, without having the emotional experience connected to an intellectual insight, clients will not change much:

> Determining the importance of affect in the change process, and noting how the affective interplay between therapist and patient facilitates or hinders the analytic process, is a huge task. It is also a necessary one. For example, in my clinical experience I have observed that the patients who seem to change the most are those who are capable of deep grieving, that is, crying profusely or sobbing. Patients who achieve equal levels of insight without this profound affective experience do not change to the same degree. I have to admit that I do not understand why this might be true, yet I believe it is. (ibid: 16)

Emotional engagement of the therapist

However, the therapeutic process is not just about the client re-living emotional experiences in the presence of the therapist. The therapist forms part of the process and is part of the client's currently lived emotional experience. Furthermore, the therapist will be having his or her own emotional experience of the client and the relationship. Maroda argues that therapists should engage in a *mutual* emotional relationship with the client. She suggests that therapists should not only allow themselves to be emotionally engaged with and touched by the client but also that therapists should disclose their own emotional responses to the client. She suggests that the most beneficial therapeutic exchanges involve the *mutual* expression of deep feeling:

> The essence of mutuality lies in the analyst's co-participation and emotional honesty, not in the unequivocal sharing of the patient's experience. (ibid: 29)

She suggests that patients try to stimulate emotional responses in therapists (maybe unconsciously) and that therapists should disclose such responses to complete the communication and help the client articulate that which is too difficult for them to understand or articulate yet. She suggests that if the client is stimulating an emotional response in the therapist, the client needs to know that he or she has succeeded in doing so. This is especially so in relation to feelings that go beyond words and which may therefore relate to pre-verbal experiences. Maroda is referring specifically to the phenomenon of countertransference – by which she means emotional responses evoked in the analyst related to both the patient's history and the analyst's. As such, although the emotional engagement is very much a 'here and now' experience, it relates specifically to historical emotional material.

Other approaches, such as humanistic and existential approaches, reject the notion of unconscious transference and countertransference, suggesting that all experience is real, available to consciousness and currently lived. Within these approaches there is an emphasis on therapists being authentic or congruent – that is, acting and using words in accordance with how they are *feeling*. Rogers suggested that congruence meant always acting as a therapist in accordance with how he was feeling, so that, if he was feeling angry and critical with a client, he found it unhelpful to act calmly and pleasantly (1961). Rogers (1969) believed that congruence was the most important of his three core relationship conditions, and that it was only once the therapist was real, and could be perceived as such, that the other conditions (empathy and unconditional positive regard) could be effective. For Rogers, congruence and acceptance of feelings was directly linked to client change. Paradoxically he found that the more he was willing to just be himself and accept the complexities of the other, the more change seemed to be stirred up:

> It is a very paradoxical thing – that to the degree that each one of us is willing to be himself, then he finds not only himself changing; but he finds that other people to whom he relates are also changing. At least this is a very vivid part of my experience, and one of the deepest things I think I have learned in my personal and professional life. (ibid: 22)

Rogers found that when he was really congruent, really present in the therapeutic encounter, he acted in surprising and unusual ways.

Again, I found this to be the case in my own research. When therapists set aside their 'therapist' stance, and allowed themselves to respond congruently and emotionally in the moment, this proved incredibly helpful for clients. For example, one therapist burst into tears on hearing that the client was having to end the therapeutic relationship. She had been cautious and concerned about whether this was the right thing to do and whether it made her a not-very-good therapist. However, the tears evoked in the client her own emotional response: like a shutter coming up the client was able to experience and express her own tears and sobbing at the pain connected to the experience. This client became aware of her own deeply buried feeling of not mattering to anyone – a feeling about which she had been previously unaware. This experience marked a huge change and shift in the work.

More interestingly perhaps, though, there seemed to be more than one emotional process or level going on at the same time. At the level of the therapeutic work, there was a conscious, articulated emotional engagement between client and therapist, and at this level both client and therapist were able to engage with all emotional responses, including difficult and negative ones. The client's experiences were often familiar and might, therefore, be described as 'transference'. They were invariably either conscious or brought into consciousness through the course of the therapy, and usually articulated. However, there also seemed to be another, non-verbal emotional level operating at the same time. At this deeper emotional level, which was much more hidden, the client had a reliable and perceptive emotional part of herself that experienced the therapist and the relationship accurately. At this level the client was aware that the therapist cared for her and was also aware of things that she could not consciously 'know'. For example, in one pair, the therapist had a similar background to the client, which meant that she felt particularly connected to the client and understood the client's story in a very particular way. She had never disclosed that she had a similar background to the client. However, the client revealed that it was important to her to be understood by this particular therapist because of their similar backgrounds. When I questioned her as to what she meant about them having similar backgrounds, she wasn't able to answer. Of course she couldn't – the therapist had never verbally or consciously disclosed this information to the client! However, at some subliminal, emotional level, the client just knew that they had similar backgrounds. This knowledge was emotional knowledge, not cognitive knowledge.

Similarly in another pair, there was a very high correlation between how they both experienced a particular session. At one point in the session the client had smiled, and recounted to me what the smile meant to him and what it signified. When I spoke to the therapist about the same session she too mentioned the smile and then proceeded to say what she thought it meant to the client – and reproduced the exact list of things that the client had mentioned! Neither of them had spoken about the smile in the session or subsequently and yet clearly there was a lot being communicated in it – not verbally, consciously, but non-verbally, subliminally, emotionally.

Conclusion

We have seen that there is a body of literature, from diverse models, which suggests that what takes place on an emotional level within therapy is significant in respect of client change. There is literature to suggest that emotion and cognition are separate but intertwined processes but that emotion is more powerful – and that it is therefore this level that therapy needs to address primarily. This is seen as being done within a mutual emotional engagement between client and counsellor, with both parties having emotional experiences of each other in the therapeutic 'here and now'.

However, there is other literature that suggests that, simultaneous with this mutual emotional engagement, there is a deeper emotional current that is more subliminal or non-verbal and that what happens at this level is also a significant factor in a successful therapy. This deeper emotional current is often not articulated within the therapy and at times what passes between client and counsellor at this level *cannot* be 'known' cognitively. There seems to be evidence that not only is there a different kind of knowing to the cognitive knowing – a more subliminal, emotional knowing – but that it is this emotional level that needs attention. It is at this level that the therapeutic relationship forms and allows therapeutic work to be done and it is at this level that change happens. Emotional knowledge is often unseen and neglected – by its very nature it is elusive and sometimes outside of our awareness. It is often unknown and only becomes known by stepping into uncertainty. It cannot be rationally explained. How can the client who did not consciously know that her therapist had the same background to her explain how she nevertheless 'knew' this to be the case? How can a therapist 'know' what a client's smile meant when the client did not communicate this to the therapist verbally? The knowledge described is emotional knowledge – a mysterious yet powerful communication, a different kind of knowing that nevertheless, if paid attention to, can provide valuable information. In the West we tend to attach value to rational knowledge and are suspicious of anything that cannot be 'proved'. However, emotional knowledge has an ongoing effect on our everyday lives and plays a vital role in growth and change. Rather than immediately discounting what we cannot rationally know, perhaps it is important to step into a more unknowing frame of mind – a place where we can allow ourselves to become aware of a deeper emotional, intuitive knowledge. If we are able to access that knowledge and pay attention to it, deeper change may be facilitated.

References

Beck, A.T. (1976) *Cognitive Therapy and the Emotional Disorders*, International Universities Press

Damasio, A.R. (2000) *The Feeling of What Happens*, Random House

Denzin, N.K. (1984) *On Understanding Emotion*, Jossey-Bass

Deurzen, E. van. (2002) *Existential Counselling and Psychotherapy in Practice*, 2nd edition, Sage Publications

Gendlin, E.T. (1996) *Focusing-Oriented Psychotherapy*, Guilford Press

____ (1997) *Experiencing and the Creation of Meaning – A Philosophical and Psychological Approach to the Subjective*, Northwestern University Press

Greenberg, L.S. & Paivio, S.C. (2003) *Working With Emotions in Psychotherapy*, Guilford Press

Greenberg, L.S., Rice, L.N. & Elliott, R. (1993) *Facilitating Emotional Change – The Moment-by-Moment Process*, Guilford Press

Laing, R.D. (1990) *The Divided Self*, Penguin Books

Langs, R. (1995) *Clinical Practice and the Architecture of the Mind*, H Karnac

LeDoux, J. (1998) *The Emotional Brain*, Orion Books

Maroda, K.J. (1998) *Seduction, Surrender, and Transformation: Emotional Engagement in the Analytic Process*, The Analytic Press

____ (2004) *The Power of Counter-Transference: Innovations in Analytic Technique*, The Analytic Press

Rogers, C.R. (1961) *On Becoming a Person*, Houghton Mifflin

____ (1969) 'Two Divergent Trends' in May, R. (ed.) *Existential Psychology*, McGraw-Hill, pp 84-92

Sartre, J-P. *Being and Nothingness*, trans. Hazel E. Barnes (Routledge Classics, 2003), first published in French, 1943

Scott, M.J. & Dryden, W. (2003) 'The cognitive-behavioural paradigm' in Wolfe, R., Dryden, W. & Strawbridge, S. (eds.) *Handbook of Counselling Psychology*, Sage Publications

Smith, D.L. (1991) *Hidden Conversations*, H. Karnac

Spinelli, E. (1993) 'The unconscious: an idea whose time has gone?' *Journal of Society for Existential Analysis, 4*, pp.217-247

____ (1994) 'Riding shotgun for Freud or aiming a gun at his head? A reply to David L. Smith.' *Journal of Society for Existential Analysis*, 5, pp.157-165

Strasser, F. (1999) *Emotions – Experiences in Existential Psychotherapy and Life*, Gerald Duckworth

Buddhist Psychology, Therapy and Not-Knowing

Caroline Brazier

Give me the faith
To have doubt
And the clarity
To see my confusion

In the moment of encounter we do not know. The peril of that moment is that we inevitably search into our store of memory and mental constructs for meaning rather than enquiring of the encounter itself. In the process of such searching for meaning we deform and limit perception, and yet it is the search for meaning which leads us to look, and look again.

Alternatively we search external authorities for answers. Knowing our own inadequacy, or greedy for more than we have, we hand to the other the source of knowledge and stop seeking answers in our own experience at all. We look to the master to provide what we desire, enslaving our attention in the framework of another's concepts.

The mind is a mirror and so is the mind's world. Even in our attention to others, we see the reflective veneer of our own projections; our ego-driven assumptions. We expect of others the certainty that we long for, or the ignorance that we fear. We do not hear the other in their voices, but make them a mouthpiece for our disowned views.

Modern thinking is complicated on the matter of truth. On the one hand, it places scientific enquiry and measurable outcomes on the plinth of verity. On the other it bids us reject external authority and come back to the self as the only valid reference point. Apparent opposites, objective and subjective, are uncomfortable bed-fellows, yet at a simplistic level such choices have one thing in common: an abhorrence of not-knowing.

Not-knowing can be spacious. It can allow for subtle exploration of nuance and tone. It can expand enquiry and give it eloquence. At the same time not-knowing can become a backwater where a person might uncommittedly shuffle between interpretations. A postmodern indulgence of complication, not-knowing can become a game of hide and seek in which concepts become shadows and mirrors and nothing is knowable. Refusal to know can be as pernicious and fundamentalist as naïve certainties. How, then, can we stay in a place of not-knowing without the not-knowing, in itself, becoming a dogma?

Unanswerable Questions and Ignorance

"But how can you not want to know where we came from? How can you have a religion that doesn't tell you about the creation?" The young man was insistent as he fixed me in his impassioned gaze. He was a young Muslim cleric, liberal and smartly dressed in Western style, and certain in his faith. To him, the Buddhist ideas I had been explaining to the multi-faith group made no sense.

I paused, unsure what to say. It wasn't the question itself which unnerved me so much as the tone of it, which combined confidence with a kind of desperation. Answers which I would have given on my home turf felt much harder to justify or explain here in his territory. I found myself responding with what now seemed rather inadequate and weak arguments as I struggled to explain the importance of 'not knowing' the answers to these questions and putting my attention on other things. Against his surety, my Buddhist agnosticism about the origins of our existence felt wishy-washy and less than satisfactory. A level of certainty about uncertainty slipped away. Perhaps that is why the experience has stuck with me since. None of us likes to feel inadequate or weak.

Reflecting on the exchange, however, clarifies something about the nature of Buddhist thought. Buddhism does not concern itself so much with matters of belief as with the process of enquiry. Sure enough, the enquiry isn't just an unformed meander through cluttered mind-spaces or a game of balancing angels on points of emptiness. It has an intended end point – the eradication of the mental fog which comes from trying to make the world conform to our conscious and unconscious agendas, for example – but it does not come with the intent of finding certainties about the nature of the universe, material or otherwise.

Unlike the religion of my Muslim colleague, Buddhism does not generally address metaphysical questions. The Buddha himself declined to provide answers to questions of the sort that my Muslim companion asked. In this at least I should feel in good company. The Buddha indeed taught that such questions were not conducive to the spiritual path. They were lines of enquiry which distracted one from the real purpose of the spiritual life. Trying to answer such questions would simply get us into a false position, clutching at concepts we could not grasp.

In the Buddhist texts, the suttas, we find a list of unanswerable questions. This list includes questions about the origins or extent of the universe as well as ones about what is going to happen to the Buddha himself after he dies[1]. The Buddha advised his followers not to get trapped into pursuing these matters and remained silent when questioned upon them.

The Buddha's unanswerable questions have given rise to much reflection over the years. For example, they are discussed by John Hick (2004), the theologian and philosopher. Hick uses the questions to support his argument that there is as much need for a 'theory of religious ignorance' as there is for one of religious knowledge. Ignorance, he says, is important because it acknowledges our human limits and opens us up to the possibility that we do not have the capacity to know everything about the processes behind the universe. Spiritual truth may be greater than anything we can envisage. Buddhism, Hick suggests, offers one framework for understanding this theological not-knowing.

Not-Knowing and *Avidya*

There is not-knowing and there is ignorance. At a superficial level, the Buddha's appreciation of the importance of not delving into areas which are beyond the human sphere of knowledge can seem at odds with his teachings on ignorance. It is an apparent paradox of Buddhist thought that, on the one hand, many of those subject areas which religions commonly address are left unexplored, whilst, at the same time, the tradition's main focus is on dispelling ignorance. The Buddhist conceptualisation of the spiritual task, as set out in the teaching known as the Four Noble Truths, suggests that human suffering arises out of our desire to escape from the more uncomfortable aspects of reality. In particular, the teaching notes that we avoid experiencing affliction, *dukkha*, in general, and particularly the recognition of our nature as mortal beings, subject to sickness, ageing and disappointment, by indulging our cravings for sensory distractions and 'becoming'. As a result of ordinary life anxieties arising from these ordinary stresses, humans develop illusory states of mind, trying to diminish fears and create a sense of permanence, despite knowing that their lives are all

[1] This list appears in two suttas: Majjhima Nikaya 63 and 72

too finite. In particular humans 'become' by asserting their own solid identities, using life events and adventitious experience to create stories in which they take leading roles. They also distract themselves by dwelling on unanswerable questions and ruminating on unproductive thoughts rather than seeing what is evident.

The illusion of stability which is created through clinging to delusory ideas and unproductive thought patterns is referred to as *avidya,* which literally means 'not seeing' and is commonly translated as ignorance. *Avidya* is the limited mind that holds onto dogmatic belief systems and opinions. The mind is conditioned by *avidya.* It clings to ideas of continuity and security. The senses are conditioned by *avidya.* The eye sees familiarity, seeking out comforting landmarks in the unowned world of objective reality. The ear listens for reassurance and hears it even when none is forthcoming. The imagination is conditioned by *avidya.* It conjures stories about the nature of things to reassure itself with its own importance. *Avidya* narrows our experience. It shuts down options. Ultimately it leads to paralysis.

The two kinds of not-knowing found in Buddhist teachings thus sit in relationship to one another. The ordinary mind of *avidya* arises out of fear. We fear our mortality and powerlessness over matters of life and death. Ultimately we fear the unknown immensity of the cycles of existence and non-existence and the space beyond time. So our small-minded ignorance, the not-seeing process of *avidya,* comes out of our fear of the vast unknown spaces of birth, death and impermanence. It is these which feed the impulse to cling.

Spiritual Wisdom: Beyond Knowing

Beyond *avidya,* there arises wisdom. The Buddhist word commonly translated as wisdom is *prajna,* which more literally might be translated as 'knowing into' or 'knowing through'. This refers to a subtle and complex appreciation of phenomena, a deep penetration into the space beyond ordinary knowing.

In Majjhima Nikaya 72, we find the unanswerable questions listed. In this text, however, we discover that, although he discourages pursuit of the questions, the Buddha does not exactly leave them unaddressed. Vacchagotta, a wandering monk, asks the Buddha to give his views on a number of matters. He asks about the nature of the cosmos, the person of the Buddha and his fate after death. The Buddha refuses to agree with any of the propositions which Vachagotta offers, despite the fact that Vachagotta covers all the logical possibilities. Answers to these questions, the Buddha suggests, are beyond speculative views or human logic. They cannot be known through intellectual analysis.

To answer such questions would require the transcendence of conceptual thought. It would need one to stand on ground that has no ground, the space which the unenlightened mind does not have. This ground of no-ground can only be reached by going beyond *avidya* and discovering a different kind of seeing, freed from self-interested concerns about existence and continuity. It would be like stepping through the looking-glass into a new world. If one could look into experience in this new way, a different kind of consciousness would emerge, but from the standpoint of ordinary view, this consciousness is pretty unfathomable.

> Of course you're befuddled, Vaccha. Of course you're confused. Deep, Vaccha, is this phenomenon, hard to see, hard to realise, tranquil, refined, beyond the scope of conjecture, subtle, to-be-experienced by the wise. For those with other views, other practices, other satisfactions, other aims, other teachers, it is difficult to know. (Aggi-Vacchagotta Sutta)

Reflecting on the conversation with the young Muslim, I see that our different approaches to questions of creation and teleology reflect differences of assumption which are made by our respective religious traditions regarding the status of knowledge. As a Buddhist, I follow a teaching which says that the attempt to find certainty about such questions would involve the kind of grasping mentality which is the root cause of all human problems. Not being enlightened, I cannot stand on groundlessness. I cannot find the answers, and to imagine that I can would be grandiosity.

Buddhism describes a path, not a destination. The Buddhist teachings are described as a raft to cross the river[2]; a finger pointing to the moon[3], but the other shore and the moon are not defined. Our ultimate destination is alluded to in imagery, not concretised in definition, because it is too 'difficult to know'. For this reason, Buddhism might be termed a 'religion of ignorance'.

Buddhism is often considered an apophatic tradition; a *via negativa*, or negative route of enquiry. In following the Buddhist path, we hold to the place of not-knowing lest we are drawn into the false creations of certainty which congeal into the defensive edifice of the ordinary psyche. There is no resting

---

[2] The simile of the raft appears in Majjhima Nikaya 22.

[3] An image used by Nagarjuna among others.

place. In the words of the Heart Sutra, core of the Prajna Paramita traditions, we are always *going, going, going beyond. Always going beyond. Awakening*[4].

Nor is the question of not-knowing strange to Hick's own religious tradition. There is an apophatic strand within Christianity, commonly associated with its mysticism, which emphasises the unknowability of God. Christian mystical writings, such as *The Cloud of Unknowing*[5], express a view of God or the divine presence that cannot be directly known through human capacities. The ineffable can only be experienced indirectly and interpreted through symbolic representation.

This is an idea not dissimilar to that of Dharmakaya[6] in Buddhism. According to the Three Bodies Teaching[7], there is an absolute expression of Buddha-ness, referred to as the Dharmakaya. This embodiment of the central mystery is only approached indirectly through esoteric practices and through its incarnate manifestation as the historical Buddha, known as the Nirmanakaya, and its spiritual expression in the form of the multiple representations of celestial Buddhas and Bodhisattvas. These latter beings embody the essence of Buddha in forms which take on an intermediary state between the mystery and the mundane, known as the Sambhogakaya. The Three Bodies Teaching describes ways of knowing the unknowable. It describes the clothing of formless essence in material, metaphoric and symbolic forms, which provide bridges to the unknowable, whilst at the same time themselves embodying the infinite.

Textures of Not-Knowing

Whilst human process happens within a spacious field of uncertainty, the landscape is not without features. It has texture and depth. Sarah Maitland (2008) describes how silence is a slippery concept. The more you explore it, the harder it is to define. Like not-knowing, silence is often thought to be

---

[4] The mantra at the close of the Heart Sutra: *gate gate pāragate pārasaṃgate bodhi svāhā.*

[5] An anonymous work of Christian mysticism written in the late 14th century.

[6] The ultimate essence of Buddha, which can only be known when manifest in human or spiritual form.

[7] The Three Bodies Teaching, which is widely used in the Mahayana traditions, explains the experience of Buddha in terms of three levels of existence. Put simply, these can be understood as: the ultimate; the symbolic and the incarnate: Dharmakaya, Sambhogakaya and Nirmanakaya.

defined by absence, but this definition does not do justice to the feeling tone of the experience. Maitland says:

> I increasingly realise there is an interior dimension to silence, a sort of stillness of heart and mind which is not a void but a rich space. (ibid: 26)

In a similar way, not-knowing has texture and depth. Some not-knowing is fear-based and tight, but other not-knowing is grand and laden with potential. Some is light and sun-filled, while other is dark and brooding. Within the spaces where conclusion is held back, intuition of structure emerges within the nebulous. Lightly held senses of process and colouration flow through the experiencing; shadows against the brilliance of unclouded being. In these, reflections of wisdom emerge.

With time and experience one comes to rely more on kinds of knowing which go beyond words. The felt sense (Gendlin, 1981) can generally be trusted more than the cognitive insight. This deep intuition is particularly ethical. When asked what he wants, a person may waver. When asked what is right, he usually knows. Such instinctual certainty seems to come from beyond the ego. The conscience like a compass points towards the ethical. It speaks in the silence between our inner voices.

In meditation we listen for the spaces in which conscience and Buddha-mind can arise. We watch the arising of breath and the falling away thereof, and in between it we find the stillness. We observe the fleeting impressions of thoughts against a background of silence whose depths, we sense, have a pile, deep as velvet. We peel back layer on layer of reaction, each obscuring the next, drawn in by a faintly glimmering spaciousness which we sense behind them. What is it that we seek? Fast as we try to grasp it, the emptiness dissolves into thought.

There is a present-ness in this not-knowing. The emptiness of Buddhism is a fullness of Dharmakaya. It is the experience of primaeval awe which wonders at everything but does not know anything. Such experiences might be considered in terms of what Hick (2004) refers to as *The Real*. They are not knowable in ordinary, cognitive, terms, yet are experienced in a way which, to the person experiencing them, can be profoundly transformative.

Not-Knowing and Therapeutic Process

Can we ever know another? Each of us remains a mystery even to ourselves, so what hope for an understanding of another person during the fleeting encounter of the therapy hour? When I sit with a client, I do not know what lies behind the words they speak. I do not understand the associations buried in the story they bring or the meaning of events or characters in it. Neither do they. This is probably why they have come. These are things for us to tease out together. Therapy is a dance with not-knowing; a venture towards the mystery which lies behind the ever-receding mirage of certainty. It is a compromise with uncertainty. Sense may emerge as the chaotic kaleidoscope of experience is shuffled and reshuffled, but this sense is always provisional.

Thirty years ago as a young trainee counsellor I spent many hours in personal therapy reviewing my childhood and adolescence and building stories about the meaning of my life. The truth which I uncovered at that time served me well in the context of my life then. It contributed to changes which I made and gave me insight which helped me to build confidence and develop new and enriching capacities both in my personal life and in my work. Now, perhaps with the wisdom of approaching age, or maybe simply because the kaleidoscope has turned again, the events and experiences that coloured those earlier insights look different. People whom I judged back then, I now look on with greater understanding and kindness. Insights I gained about causes and intentions have mellowed with shifting identifications. As an older woman I have greater understanding for the teachers and parents whom I once criticised. I have been there too. Life has shifted the scales and re-coloured the lens through which I view others. Truth is not absolute but situational.

Working from a Buddhist perspective, I am aware that questions relating to what can and cannot be known arise when I am engaged with the client just as much as they do in religious practice. Part of the therapeutic art involves developing awareness of what line of enquiry is likely to be profitable to the person in fostering their mental and spiritual health (for are the two truly different in kind?). Where should we put our attention in order to deepen our understanding instead of clouding it with prejudices? What is true and what is delusional?

Therapy is a pursuit of truth, but chasing answers can be a pitfall. Clients frequently arrive preoccupied with big questions and struggling with dilemmas about the direction and nature of their life journey. Sometimes the dilemmas are pressing, linked to immediate events and forthcoming decisions or integrating painful memories from the past. Other times, though, like the unanswerable questions that the Buddha posed, the things that preoccupy a client are simply acting as distractions from other more significant insights and decisions. The process of worrying about things which may never happen, or agonising over past mistakes can be part of a pattern of avoiding *dukkha*. It occupies the mind, drawing attention away from matters which may be more important to the person's psychological well-being.

In Buddhist psychology, the perceiving mind is viewed as one of the senses, capable of being drawn into processes of clinging and attachment, maintaining the state of *avidya*. The futile pursuit of unanswerable questions can simply be a sense attachment, the mind faculty masking our deep despair by grasping at easy worries. Buddhism lists restless worry and doubt among the hindrances to spiritual practice[8], and these qualities often manifest in the troubled client. They are symptomatic of the unproductive procrastination we are describing.

Nor do these doubts facilitate a deconstruction of the false perceptions that Buddhist psychology identifies as the root problem in the human psyche. Far from questioning the real factors in a situation, self-doubt is generally grounded in a kind of surety about the identity and the self-story, albeit a negative one. Rather than a real enquiry into his life circumstances, the client, locked in compulsive agonising, confirms and reconfirms his hopeless position, leaving no room for change.

It would be wrong, however, to think of the ordinary sense of identity and the search for familiarity which all of us engage in as something to be eliminated in therapy. This would be unrealistic. In everyday situations, the self is functional. Buddhism talks of relative or provisional truth. For example, *The Lotus Sutra*, perhaps the most important Mahayana text, offers the parable of the *Apparitional City*[9]. This story describes how weary travellers, approaching a magical city, are encouraged to think they are arriving at their final destination. They are elated and find new energy to complete the journey. After resting, however, the group discover that, far from having arrived, they have to continue onwards to reach their real destination. The illusory city is just a staging post, conjured up in order to give them hope, but only part way along the path to their journey's end. The constructs of the mind provide such staging posts. They are illusions, but yet, provided they are not too rigid or too negative, they help us to function in a world where everything is impermanent and subject to changing conditions.

---

[8] The five hindrances are: sense desire, ill will, sloth and torpor, restless worry and doubt.

[9] Lotus Sutra Chapter 7

Partial truth is often easier to hear than full-blown reality. We filter experience in order to make it palatable. Insights in therapy are generally partial or approximate. They serve well enough for the time being, offering a foundation from which a person may appraise their life and find new energy for living it.

Diagnosis and the Space between Fear and Function

As we recognise things, we name them. Naming asserts limits and establishes ownership. By giving an object verbal status, I fit it into my world and define its parameters. I take control of it. The mind names experience in order to feel safe. Diagnosis is a particular example of naming. Giving the pain a label like 'indigestion' or 'muscle ache', 'toothache' or 'rheumatism', we ring-fence it. We limit its capacity to invade the imagination. We take it out of the shadowy world of uncertainty and render it tamed, at least to some degree, by the constraint of language. But naming is a device, a partial truth and sometimes a straightjacket.

Buddhism refers to the process of naming. The term *nama-rupa*, means named form[10]. It describes a phenomenon which is part of the cycle of clinging and attachment by which we create the identity. The process of naming reduces a complex object or an experience to a unit which can be described by one word, and, in so doing, places it in a mental box. It creates a feeling of familiarity and safety in an uncertain and infinitely complicated situation.

At a professional level, in psychotherapy, naming and diagnosis are given status because they help to define the therapeutic process. Whilst therapeutic change rests upon holding open the place of uncertainty, in the therapy world, as in many areas of modern life, diagnosis and measurement have been given increasing importance. This has mixed value. One of the problems of a system based on diagnosis is that it tends to create false pockets of certainty. However tentative the categorisation which is made, once declared, the diagnostic assumption becomes a Procrustean bed onto which both client and therapist will tend to fit their observations. Often clients come with a diagnosis already attached. Either imposed by a previous encounter, or, commonly, self-determined, it becomes a frame onto which

---

[10] The translation and interpretation of this term is somewhat controversial, but I have argued elsewhere (2003) that it represents the process of identification of an object prior to sense attachment.

an account of events is cobbled. Such diagnoses are at best approximations of complex situations, and often smoke-screens for less acceptable versions of the as yet undiscovered truth.

At the same time, the false assumptions on which people base their sense of ordinary reality are sometimes necessary for them to function. Not-knowing can be spacious, but this is not always comfortable. In the space between experience and diagnosis the mind can play all manner of strange games. Who has not known the fear of waking in the night with a strange symptom and conjuring anxieties in their imagination? The demons of imminent mortality can ride high in the wee small hours. Diagnosis can reassure. The condition has a name, a cause and a treatment. Even when the news is grave, people will often say 'at least I know now what I'm up against'.

Recognition and Identification

Enquiry may be essential to the therapeutic process and to healthy living, but it needs a framework in which to operate. Not-knowing can be limiting if we have no reference points for understanding our experience. Whilst we do not know anything in totality, without some kind of recognition, the world feels flat and uninteresting or chaotic and confused. With no hooks for the intellect, the attention switches off. If we don't know anything, we don't have questions to ask and stop being curious. Recognition directs our attention and focuses our intention. This knowledge provides windows through which we can look at things more clearly.

When I was visiting Buddhist friends in Hawaii a few years ago, I had the opportunity to snorkel in some tide ponds. To my amazement, despite their small size, these pools were full of tropical fish of many different colours and shapes. The experience was very exciting, but with no knowledge of the subject, to my untrained eye the many small creatures swimming around me were simply labelled 'fish'.

The second day I went swimming in the tide pools again, but this time I was accompanied by my friend, who was a marine biologist. She brought with her guidebooks which helped me to identify the species of fish which we saw. With the ability to distinguish between the different varieties, my perception became far sharper and the whole experience more enjoyable. I looked for features and recalled images I had seen. My attention was focused.

As we gain knowledge and enthusiasm for a subject, we see the things which relate to it more richly. The world gains depth in that particular respect because we are encouraged to be curious about it in very specific ways. To the birdwatcher, a flock of water birds is diverse and can hold his attention all day, as he names species and studies behaviour. The casual passer-by, on the other hand, just sees ducks or gulls.

Naming things makes us look more carefully. The process of identification provides a lens through which to view the world accurately and with intention. Buddhist meditations which involve precise analyses of mind states and elements similarly help the practitioner to observe experience more sharply. The teachings on mindfulness[11] describe how a practitioner, stretching out his arm, knows that he is stretching out his arm; breathing in a breath, knows that he is breathing in a breath. In the detail of the observation, he notices the arising of the action, dependent upon conditions and the ending of the same action, also dependent upon conditions. The simple observation of the constructed nature of the action, and its temporality, take the meditator into the heart of the Buddha's insight. He has direct sensate awareness of dependence and impermanence. Mindfulness is recollection of Dharma, the bottomless truth.

Naming experience and bringing detailed awareness to bear on it provides a lens through which vistas of spaciousness emerge. Labelling the flower directs attention, supports curiosity about its nature and this curiosity invites a deeper penetration into new emergent questions about its flower essence. What does it mean to smell a rose? The scent is beyond words, but if we do not recognise the rose we probably will not smell it at all.

Road Blocks to Knowing

Not-knowing is not always spacious. Sometimes it becomes deadness. It can be the bottom of the heap when all inspiration has been exhausted. How many times have I sat trying to write, with words just not appearing, and an empty screen in front of me? Have you ever suffered from writer's block? Words disappear. All that is left is a blank space. There is nothing to say. No thoughts. No opinions.

This absence is not the ecstatic experience of the mystics or even the dark night of the soul. It has no depth, no subtlety of nuance. It is just grey nothingness; a state of *avidya* in which the mind contracts down to near

---

[11] The Satipatthana Sutta describes the establishment of the foundations of mindfulness.

complete closure. Entering intellectual hibernation, a shutter comes down over our awareness so that all we can see is blankness.

In a text known as the Ant Hill Sutta[12] the Buddha analyses a dream presented by a monk. In the dream, on the instruction of a passing deva, the monk digs into an ant hill and pulls out a series of objects one by one. Interpreting the dream, the Buddha suggests that the ant hill represents the psyche, and the objects are obstructions to the spiritual journey which are to be eliminated. The first object to be pulled out of the ant hill is a bar. According to the Buddha's interpretation, this bar, which was symbolic of the wooden barrier across the entrance to a village at that time, represented a complete refusal to look at oneself. The village barrier prevented intruders. It barred entry. So too, the mind sometimes creates blocks, preventing thoughts or responses from emerging, and stopping us in our tracks.

When the mind is so closed, it is hard for any line of enquiry to loosen our thoughts or influence our perception of others. We become tongue-tied. Nothing goes in and nothing comes out. The mind clings to nothingness lest other more frightening possibilities be allowed into our thoughts.

Therapy as Curiosity

Therapy is an encounter with what we cannot know. It is not, or should not be, the pseudo-doubt of rumination. It implicitly brings into question the processes of mental clinging, and the emotional triggers which are driving them. Like scientific enquiry, therapy often involves testing propositional statements against reality, in as much as it can be surmised. The primary quality that the therapist brings to the encounter, then, is curiosity. All else flows from this attribute. Compassion, wisdom and empathic listening all flow from curiosity. Without curiosity, none of these can arise. If I am not interested in my client, his world and how he sees it, I will neither care for him nor offer a helpful relationship. Curiosity is the expression of not-knowing. It is the out-stretched hand that meets the other. Once I believe that I know the answers, I stop investigating. I become lazy and rest on assumptions. At this point the therapeutic relationship dies.

Fixity of view which gives rise to a desire to package and define experience is the primary source of psychological problems. As a result of unnamed fears, people live with a compulsion to create stories and, as a result, narrow perception and live in a personal world of preconceptions:

---

[12] Majjhima Nikaya 23

avidya. The self-story offers a place to hang unsettling anomalies of behaviour and unexplained mood swings. It helps people avoid getting in too deep. If the therapist reinforces the compulsive script by accepting this story at face value, it can simply add more rigidity to the confining psychic structures. Holding such stories lightly and enquiring into them with curiosity lays a foundation for a more authentic way of being. At the same time, we do not know the truth of the client's life, or the horrors held at bay by such fictions. Good therapists tread gently and respectfully, inviting interest and a loosening of the certainties without imposing or destroying.

In fact, curiosity is not only important in the therapist. It is also a primary outcome agenda for the client. Someone who is capable of curiosity is open to life. Watching children at play, we know that their development is healthy when they are full of interest in their surroundings. As they grow, they may become more wary, less free and less exploratory, searching out an identity in which to hide and a niche within the crowd. They respond to constraints of adults and the conditions of worth (Thorne, n.d.), which inevitably arise as part of ordinary or problematic parenting. As adults, less bound to living within others' agendas, people tend to settle into lives of familiarity and constriction. Even the person who is unhappy, or lives in an abusive situation, may fear change more than continuity.

The person who joins me in my consulting room is, and always will be, mysterious to me. The world they describe, conveyed in stories and reflected in behaviour, hovers before us as an assembly of ghostly others. We can visit this spectral world but we cannot know it in any absolute sense. My job is to be curious and, in doing so, to invite my client's curiosity to grow and expand. For this to happen, fear needs to dissipate enough so that the tightly held beliefs and interpretations which protect the client's sense of self can be suspended. We need to relax into not-knowing.

We do not need to hold the answers in order to be helpful to our clients. What is needed is deep fascination with life and an intention to remain curious even when clarity seems to emerge. We need to trust the wisdom in the silence. One only has to look at the variety of therapies on offer in modern times to realise that no one system has a fool-proof response to human process. Therapy is the relationship of accompaniment in which the therapist works with the client in order to explore the panorama of their life. It is a shared journey into the unknown, for neither therapist nor client knows the territory with any certainty.

References

'Aggi-Vacchagotta Sutta: To Vacchagotta on Fire' (MN 72), translated from the Pali by Thanissaro Bhikkhu. Access to Insight (Legacy Edition), 30 Nov. 2013, www.bit.ly/notknowing03

Brazier, C. (2003) *Buddhist Psychology*, Constable-Robinson

Gendlin, E. (1981) *Focusing* 2nd ed., Bantam

Hick, J. (2004) *The Buddha's Undetermined Questions and the Religions* www.bit.ly/notknowing02

Maitland, S. (2008) *A Book of Silence*, Granta

Thorne, Brian (2007) 'Person Centred Therapy: Historical Context and Developments in Britain' in Dryden, W. (ed.) *Dryden's Handbook of Individual Therapy* 5th edition, Sage Publications

Known Unknowns

Bob Chisholm

"There are known knowns. These are things we know that we know. There are known unknowns. That is to say, there are things that we know that we don't know. But there are also unknown unknowns. There are things we don't know we don't know."

Donald Rumsfeld

We should recall the circumstances of the US Defence Secretary's gnomic statement. It was at a press conference in 2002 prior to the invasion of Iraq and a reporter was questioning the intelligence which linked the regime of Saddam Hussein to Al Qaeda. Dismissing any doubts about the claim that these two avowed enemies were now working together as allies against the US, the eminently quotable Rumsfeld delivered his most memorable line. At the time, many people were baffled by his seemingly enigmatic remark, but its obscurity did help to conceal the absence of evidence behind an intelligence claim that would later prove to be entirely groundless. Undaunted, the reporter who had asked the question continued to press Rumsfeld for more information.

"Is this an unknown unknown? There are several unknowns there and I am just wondering if this an unknown unknown."

"I am not going to say which it is," the smirking Rumsfeld replied. He then went on to field more questions from his audience of bemused journalists.

Given what we now know about its true context, we might regard Rumsfeld's statement as an egregious example of political duplicity. While pretending to offer a careful consideration of a complex factual puzzle, he was actually concealing an unyielding determination to go to war. Much of whatever was unknown to Rumsfeld and his neo-conservative cronies about Iraq prior to the invasion was due to their wilful ignorance. And much of what was unknown to the public was due to its being withheld or fabricated by powerful leaders such as Rumsfeld. The true unknown, that is to say that which would have remained shrouded in uncertainty in spite of the most scrupulous efforts to know it, never dimmed the blazing neo-conservative certainties that Iraq must have possessed WMD, that it had been in league with Al Qaeda and that Saddam Hussein was intent upon launching attacks on America and its allies. In light of disclosures made after the war, the falsity of all of these convictions may now be considered known knowns. Yet, in spite of being a brazen public display of prevarication, Rumsfeld's statement still stands as a trenchant epistemological description of virtually any human activity in which unknown and unknowable factors are crucial in determining its ultimate outcome. Starting a new career, embarking on a long journey and falling in love are just three items on an immeasurably long list of endeavours that begin with incomplete knowledge as they launch into the unknown. War, however, represents another order of uncertainty quite apart from its social, political and economic ramifications. War involves death, the ultimate known unknown, as it were, though by calibrating casualties through such measurements as kill ratios, death in war can be categorised, predicted and tallied just like any other occurrence. Indeed, it was upon such cold calculation that the Iraq war could be rationally planned by the experts in the Pentagon who worked for Rumsfeld. But to perform such planning requires a certain desensitisation. The enemy cannot appear to be people to whom we would extend basic human sympathy or grant the dignity of their experience. They must be emptied of their humanity so that they appear like ciphers in a computer game. Thus, they must be known.

The surprising cogency of Rumsfeld's statement is what prompts this essay, though there is no admiration for the motives behind his remark. Fortunately, the interest here is in the actual nature of not-knowing rather than with the possibilities for dissimulation that not-knowing presents. Indeed, the theme of this essay is of finding the truth of not-knowing, though finding such truth is not at all the same as arriving at demonstrable facts as in a scientific inquiry or some other factual investigation. It is about reaching a provisional sort of truth, at best a limited kind of knowing based on the understanding that much will always remain unknown no matter how much becomes available as knowledge. In Rumsfeld's terms, it is about heightening awareness through known unknowns, instead of abiding complacently in known knowns and blithely ignoring the existence of unknown unknowns. Another way of expressing this is that it is about wonder as an ontological position from which meaning and values arise in an uncertain and mysterious world. It applies then to just about anything, including war, but it is psychotherapy rather than war that provides the material for this essay. War, of course, is a matter of conflict, whereas the concern of psychotherapy is the personal affliction of the client. Yet such affliction often has much in common with the conflicts that can lead to war. And just as war can develop suddenly with dreadful momentum, affliction can drive people to therapy with desperate urgency. That sense of affliction can feel total, making everything appear to arise from the unknown as a great and terrible mystery. Often, it is when that mysterious sense of affliction throbs like a toothache that people think about coming to therapy.

Long before I decided to become one myself, I went searching for a psychotherapist in the midst of an intense personal crisis. I felt as if I had been sucked into a whirlpool of depression and anxiety and I had no idea about what could be causing it or how to get out of it. I consulted four therapists in quick succession but none was able to help me. One said that I was suffering from my hurt inner child; another tried to convince me that I had been abused as a child even though I knew and protested that I hadn't been; another said I was undergoing a spiritual emergency; and the last stridently predicted that if I didn't get a grip I was going to get much worse. Not one, however, had any doubts about the truth of their explanations or said anything insightful that might have put what I was actually going through up for serious examination. Their known knowns, diverse as they were, offered little insight into what I was experiencing and it was clear to me that they were based more in their prior convictions than in the actual events of my life. Even so, my failure to find someone who would be able to listen to me without personal bias only increased my desperation that I would never be able to emerge from my crisis. Fortunately, in the fifth therapist I consulted I found someone who seemed capable of helping me.

From its inception, psychotherapy has always been likened to confession, but the consulting room is a very different space from the confessional. In the consulting room, there is no veil or screen that separates the therapist from client, though by using a couch and having the analyst sit behind the patient, psychoanalysis may achieve a somewhat similar separating effect. Most therapists today, however, face their clients and regard eye contact as a valuable, even necessary aspect of the therapeutic encounter. Whatever verbal exchange might occur in therapy, it does so in conjunction with a visual interaction that may be no less informative than the words that are spoken. For the client, the visual experience, especially in the first therapeutic session, is apt to be conditioned by an underlying feeling of anxiety. He (or she) usually feels exposed and vulnerable and looks for signs that he is being listened to sympathetically. In contrast to the therapists I had seen previously, this therapist seemed calm and attentive, analytical, yet still sympathetic. She said almost nothing, but only listened until the end of the session when she said three words that will remain with me forever: "We don't know". What she expressed in this simple, terse statement was far more than a frank admission of ignorance. It was also an acknowledgement that there would be no easy solutions, as it was made clear that not even a preliminary understanding was within immediate reach. Yet her keen attentiveness throughout the session had also assured me that what I was experiencing would not be dismissed as inscrutable, either. Indeed, her use of the pronoun "we" told me it had already become the issue that we would be able to explore together.

In spite of her claim not to know what I was going through, my psychotherapist was, I knew, remarkably astute and learned. I had little doubt that with her knowledge and experience she would not be fazed by either the intensity or the psychic contents of my crisis. I also sensed that she would not attempt to stretch my experience to fit the Procrustean bed of any theoretical model. Theory does figure importantly in the practice of psychotherapy, but it can do so either well or badly, depending on the awareness and skill of the therapist. Much of that skill consists of recognising that there will always be times when theory will not be of any use at all. Unfortunately, a therapist may still feel tempted to cling to a theory even when it does not offer any insight as it can seem to provide the security of a stable, objective perspective from which to interpret the client's condition. The danger here, however, is that theory can presume answers by pre-empting questions. The known may dismiss the unknown and the countless mysteries that loom like stars over any client's life can become obliterated by the glaring light that theory shines. Moreover, theory is not monolithic, but is a sprawling, often contradictory assortment of ideas about the self and psychological experience. While some therapists may avoid a conflict of ideas by adhering strictly to one theory or another, it is far more common for therapists to be 'integrative' and to draw pragmatically from a number of different theoretical models to suit the needs of each client. But predicting which theoretical insights will best serve the particular needs of a client is not a straightforward procedure and must always depend on the intuition of the therapist. For a therapist, knowing how is at least as important as knowing what. And knowing what one doesn't know – the known unknown – is at least as important as knowing what one does know – the known known.

It remains unclear to me if any theory could give an adequate explanation for my crisis, though it is easy to imagine a heated theoretical debate as to what caused it. My therapist avoided any theoretical explanations for what was happening to me and preferred to focus on the important events of my life and the feelings those events evoked. While certain experiences from my childhood such as a death in my family and difficulties at school were clearly factual and datable, the feelings or affects that arose from those experiences were far more conflicted, nebulous and imperfectly understood. Perhaps because there is a tendency to favour simple explanations for complex things, it would have been all too easy to suppose that some trauma which I had repressed must have been responsible for my crisis. Indeed, this is what some of my previous therapists had tried to make me to believe. Fortunately for me, but fatal for their pet certainties, no such trauma had ever happened to me. Although no less an authority than Freud argued that the psychological development of all children is inherently traumatic, trying to trace all psychological suffering to some stereotyped episode of violated innocence is surely mistaken. The power of traumatic events in childhood should not be underestimated. Many people do become deeply damaged because of what was inflicted on them as children. But the undoubted power of such traumas should not make us overlook the possibility that other, less evident factors can also be potent sources of psychological suffering. Moreover, those factors may not always match any theoretical understanding.

In fact, it remains something of a mystery to me as to why I fell so deeply into a very dark hole during my crisis. I felt terribly ashamed about something that I couldn't quite identify, yet the more I pondered the feeling the more bewildered I became. It even occurred to me that my bewilderment might have caused my shame as much as my shame seemed to cause my bewilderment. Rumination, the endless and fruitless mulling over woe, is regarded as a common symptom of anxiety and I was certainly ruminating. But what really seemed to drive my rumination was the feeling that I was being emotionally thwarted from making sense of my experience. I desperately wanted answers based on something tangible that I could grasp as factual truth. Not that there was any shortage of damning factual evidence in my life. Like most Western adults, I carried a thick portfolio labelled 'guilt' which was filled with a mental record of my life's failures, transgressions and shortcomings. But I was well acquainted with the contents of that file and had always tried to use it conscientiously in order to become a Better Person. The mystery now is why all that amassed emotional evidence should weigh so heavily in favour of the conviction that I was irredeemably horrible. Much of my torment consisted in the fact that I could find no reason for it. I simply didn't know.

Although there were certainly other factors involved, it seems obvious to me now that my intense craving to know was the most potent force in my anxiety. Whatever else was involved in my condition, my need to treat anxiety as a problem to be solved ensured that it would be a problem that would remain unsolved. But appreciating this paradox was beyond me and it required the steadying presence of my therapist for me to see this as a possibility. The skill of listening that she had demonstrated in our first session proved crucial in helping me broaden my perspective as time went on. Much of that skill was a matter of just listening, but her attentiveness went much deeper than simply paying attention to what I had to say. It was also the way she posed questions, which encouraged me to explore things that I had previously left unexamined. I understood that she was not merely looking for information in order to piece together my life history. She was also presenting me with new ways of looking at things. Each new perspective she presented brought forth the possibility of seeing my experience in a different light. But her keen attention also implied that there was no point in evading the often painful truths that emerged in the various turns of my self-examination. I knew I had to be truthful, even though I would never be able to know the truth in its entirety.

Perhaps the most important lesson I drew from therapy is that being truthful is not quite the same as being factual. Not that facts are unimportant or unrelated to the truth; it is that they are not always ascertainable. I tended to think of personal truth as a latticework of facts that was assembled by a process of putting my experiences into logical agreement with the world as I understood it. This is, indeed, a reasonably sound way of arriving at a consistent picture of the world as a field of experience; but it is no way to know oneself. For every important personal decision carries forward a sense of self that is less about facts than possibilities: not so much the known knowns, more the known unknowns. The vague sense of identity that seems to hover over every moment of self-consciousness is usually sufficient for most things. But in moments that require reflection before decision one's sense of identity may fall into radical question. It is in coming to terms with what one truly feels and truly thinks even before any factual assessment can take place that the truth of self is to be found. But it can still be agonisingly elusive.

Therapy for me did not conclude in any great personal revelation. In fact, there were no clear answers or any magic keys that allowed me to banish anxiety and depression from my life forever. There was, rather, a gradual subsidence of both afflictions over many sessions until one day I realised that I didn't need therapy any more. My therapist seemed to have reached the same conclusion even before I did. She simply nodded in agreement when I told her I couldn't think of anything more to say. She then said some rather encouraging things about the way I had been willing to face my problems. But there was never any suggestion that my problems had been permanently settled. I simply reached a point where I knew I would be able to carry on in the face of the unknown. But that was good enough.

I used to joke that I was becoming a psychotherapist because mental health was clearly a growth industry. But once I began to see clients I quickly learned that the vast number of people suffering from various forms of mental illness is no laughing matter. The exponential rise in mental illness over the past thirty years provides massive statistical evidence for what is clearly a grave social crisis. But even such staggering numbers hardly begin to convey the sense of loss and bewilderment that can take someone into therapy. Regrettably, it seems the very ideas of mental health and mental illness, indispensable though they appear, tend to flatten the feeling of individual uniqueness that is necessary for a client to make sense of his life. When we hear, for example, that someone is depressed we often simply assume that he has succumbed to one of the countless pressures of modern life and may think little more about it. But looking at someone this way doesn't tell us anything about how and why he became depressed and says nothing about the person who suffers from depression. It is as though a veil of anonymity, woven on a loom of statistical evidence, indicates the frequent occurrence of psychological suffering, but conceals the personal dimension that is the very essence of any psychological condition. Only by removing that veil to discover the actual experience of the person beneath it can psychotherapy hope to succeed. Yet, crucial though it may be for the success of therapy, such unveiling is not always welcomed by the client. Indeed, it is remarkable to me how often a client will look to the medical nomenclature of a psychiatric diagnosis in the apparent belief that this could explain his experience, not just to me as therapist, but to himself as a sufferer. It is true, of course, that prolonged or acute psychological suffering, which may include symptoms that would be familiar to any therapist or psychiatrist, can leave a client confused and desperate for definite answers. And sometimes a diagnosis does bring relief, not only by confidently identifying a problem, but also by implying that the problem can be treated, if not solved. Unfortunately, a diagnosis may also have the unwanted effect of strengthening the client's identification with it, making him feel attached to a diagnostic label that seems to grasp his personal truth, but from which he feels helpless to escape. It is almost as if some clients want to seize on a self-understanding that affords a degree of certainty even if it binds them in a tight diagnostic grip.

My training as a therapist draws heavily on Buddhist psychology, with particular emphasis on the concept of not-self. At first, the idea that at the root of all human experience there is no abiding essence or self struck me as bizarre and nonsensical. After all, if there is no self to whom could such a transcendental insight be addressed and who would be able to realise it as a truth? Moreover, most of Western philosophy, at least since Plato, has been predicated on the idea of a true self and Western psychology has largely developed by taking the idea of the self as the first axiom for understanding all personal experience. This Buddhist concept, by contrast, seemed to promote some depersonalised state of consciousness that abjures all personal vicissitudes and all interest in life in order to attain a state of unassailable tranquillity. Far from seeming to be a good way to treat mental illness, the idea of not-self appeared to prescribe a form of pathological withdrawal. In fact, not-self is not about any particular state of consciousness nor does it advocate the annihilation of personality. But it does intentionally undermine the sense of self that obtains in the notions of 'me', 'myself' and 'mine' by recognising the truth of impermanence as it pertains to human experience. While some Buddhist monks do withdraw from worldly activity in order to reach deep insight into the truth of not-self, the concept can benefit anyone in any situation in which excessive attachment has become a source of suffering. Still, not-self might seem inappropriate for someone whose self-experience is characterised by a sense of deficiency and lack. Yet, only by letting go of a sense of a self that is thought to be deficient or defective can a client begin to find better possibilities for himself.

*

When Tom came to see me, it was for anxiety attacks that seemed to come out of nowhere. A single man who had gone through a series of unsatisfying relationships, he was convinced that his inability to find the right girlfriend lay at the root of his problems. Shortly before coming to see me, he had gone to a sex therapist with his most recent girlfriend, but doing so only seemed to hasten the end of a relationship that had never been strong to begin with. Moreover, the ostensible failure of this type of therapy reinforced his doubts about his masculinity and he had begun to worry that he was actually gay. What did I think? – he wanted to know. I declined to offer an opinion, but instead asked about his feelings of sexual attraction. He began to answer before he seemed to crumple under the weight of the question. Clearly, my probing had struck a nerve of deep feeling, but it was far from clear what that feeling meant or how it contributed to his experience. Even so, the evidence of shame as he buried his face into his crossed arms was palpable. I knew I had to proceed carefully.

Shame may be understood as guilt in the form of an embodied feeling, but it may have nothing to do with culpability for any actual transgression. Indeed, just as we might call 'shameless' those who are guilty of a serious misdeed but feel no remorse for it, we can refer to those who are consumed by shame but have done nothing wrong as 'blameless'. Doing so, however, would probably do little to assuage the self-persecuting tendencies that arise out of shame, especially if the shame happens to be about sex. For sex can be a potent source of shame even when there is no attempt to act on sexual desire. The mere suggestion of an unwanted sexual desire is often sufficient to arouse a sense of guilt which may at first feel vaguely disquieting before it erupts into all-consuming shame. But the thought of a particular act or desire may not evoke shame in a straightforward causal sequence. It is more likely that the guilt-laden thought will seem to speak the truth of self by nominating itself as 'mine'. The disturbing thought of unwanted desire, shameful as it is, is not merely mental, but also claims feeling and sensation and may well have its roots in buried, forgotten layers of childhood or infantile experience. In short, shame can feel as if it is woven into the very fabric of self.

As we probed more deeply into Tom's past it became clear that the importance he placed on his sexual identity was so great as to be overwhelming. While it did seem that he was primarily attracted to women, he had never formed a strong relationship with any woman nor had he ever enjoyed a truly satisfying sexual experience with a female partner. This made him doubt his sexual orientation and threw his identity as a straight man into serious question. Although he was only curious about, rather than passionately drawn to, having sex with men, he found the idea that he might not be straight extremely disturbing. When I cautiously suggested that he might be bisexual he reacted with indignation and disbelief. He thought that bisexuality represented a compromised identity and he wondered why anyone would choose to be bisexual when it was clearly much preferable to be straight. In fact, I quickly realised that finding the right label for his sexual desire was probably not the best way to address the problem of his anxiety. Moreover, I had the uneasy feeling that Tom believed that all his concerns would fall neatly into place if only he could find a way to validate his heterosexuality. For him, everything seemed to depend on being straight and the only way he could prove this to himself was to cleave to a rigid heterosexual identity. But this meant that his self-knowledge rested largely on a symptomatic interpretation of his desires that obscured the possibility of deeper self-awareness. Tom's hunch that his panic attacks could be traced to his conflicted sexuality was certainly worth exploring. But that conflict owed at least as much to believing that a secure sense of self depended on his desires remaining safely contained within his self-image.

Possessing a secure identity is in fact an important and necessary aspect of personality. But a secure identity is not the same as a permanent one. In order to be secure, an identity must be adaptable to outer circumstances, as well as responsive to inner needs. And at its core, a truly secure identity must always engage the self-experience of the person in question in his encounters with others. But then who is that person within? As we continually examined Tom's life story, it became apparent that there was no simple answer to this question. Although the facts in his history remained consistent, each act of retrospection would cast his memories in a different light. It seemed clear that the desperation that surrounded Tom's sexual identity had its roots in his family history. The unhappy marriage of his parents weighed heavily on him from an early age, as his father had been a promiscuous philanderer and his mother had often turned to Tom to vent her frustration. She used to complain bitterly to Tom about his father and was embarrassingly frank about her husband's sexual exploits. Tom came to believe that he was somehow to blame, even though he realised that it wasn't rational for him to feel guilty for his parents' relationship. But that didn't seem to matter.

Unearthing the source of a problem is not the same as resolving it. Although Tom made great strides in coming to terms with his past and family history, he was still disturbed by his homoerotic fantasies and he still suffered occasional, if somewhat milder, anxiety attacks. Yet something had begun to shift in his experience as well. He had begun to question his belief that his sexual urges had to follow some pre-existing norm. He even began to consider the idea that sex could function as an expression of some unrecognised self-need. But most encouraging of all, he had become increasingly comfortable with things he didn't know about himself and was becoming less afraid of exploring them. Rather than desperately trying to cling to an identity that constricted his sense of self, he was beginning to question his actual experience and to look at other possibilities of thinking, feeling and living. But this was not easy for him as such reflections pointed to the necessity of making some difficult decisions. As Tom's therapist, it was my role to provide support, allowing him to explore his thoughts and feelings in the safe, uncritical shelter of my consulting room. But when he used to ask me where therapy was going to take him, I had only one reply: I didn't know.

Psychotherapy is not about providing answers for people, nor is it about encouraging them to shrug their shoulders in response to the problems they face. If anything, it is about helping them face their problems more resolutely, particularly when there are no simple or easy solutions to be found. Tom's question about where therapy was taking him applies to every client I meet. And in every case, the answer remains unknown. This is not to say that everything will always stay stuck in unmoving ignorance. But it does mean that therapy should begin with a sense of wonder about how the issues in the client's life developed as they did and how things could be different if they were to be approached differently. Although the known knowns in one's life may give a sense of stability, they may also become fixations that block a fuller awareness. They may not actually be false, but they can still mislead one into believing that they are the only things that matter. Closing one's mind around a few known facts will inevitably blind one to the possibility of finding a greater truth which must always lie in the unknown.

As a therapist I often reflect on how little I know about the lives of my clients, even though psychotherapy works within rare conditions of intimacy and trust. But therapy is inherently limited by circumstances of time and place and of what appears to be mere chance. Yet in this uncertain and limited space that therapy occupies, both therapist and client can make sense of things and try to find direction from the few things they do know in relation to the unknown; both what we know that we don't know (the known unknowns) and what we don't know that we don't know (the unknown unknowns). For it is in our relationship to the unknown that we arrive at our values, even outside of any therapeutic context. The known unknowns that Rumsfeld once presented were pseudo mysteries that were conjured by his cynical imagination. They arose from a set of false known knowns that he took for facts and then acted upon with disastrous consequences. The known unknowns that a client like Tom faces arise from the unseen depths of his being and would have the power to bring about his emotional ruin were it not for his willingness to face them. Here, at the agonised edge of being, is where psychotherapy can help someone face what he does not know, yet still finds reason to dread. The therapist may know no more about his client's possibilities than the client does, for the therapist's view into the client's world can only come through a window that the client presents. Yet by looking at the unknown together with his therapist, the client may find possibilities that he would not see otherwise. As for what they will find, that must be a known unknown which itself is ensconced in a greater surround of unknown unknowns. In the face of the unknown and the unknowable, knowing arises out of wanting to know what is truly important.

Therapy as Via Negativa

Jeff Harrison

If you don't know where you're going, any road will get you there.
To paraphrase Alice's exchange with the Cheshire Cat in
Alice in Wonderland

Absence can have great power and intrigue. When the *Mona Lisa* was stolen in 1911, visitor numbers increased. People wanted to see the space that was left behind. Only when it was returned did its status as the most famous painting in the Louvre begin.

A client, O, sits facing me. She is racked by anxiety. She does not want any clever theory from me, explanations of her feelings, interpretations of her behaviour. As she talks, I quickly realise that there are many things about herself that she does not like and accept. Her entirely understandable wish to be rid of her anxiety is merely the latest in a long line.

Who's Confused?

We have to be careful with words. Yet we use words to highlight their danger. Words – and the grammar with which we arrange them to make sense – suggest certain entities, configurations and relationships. They can reflect realities or create unrealities. They can open and close worlds and possibilities.

There are grammars of presence and absence. Absence can taunt, resonate, haunt, promise potential…

There are grammars of darkness – and of its interplay with light.

There are mysterious interactions between verbal meaning and silence. Sometimes words are inadequate or seem belated. Sometimes the taming that comes with naming is welcome; alexithymia is the distress of inscrutable symptoms.

There are grammars of selfhood. 'I don't know *where* I am' says something profoundly different from 'I don't know where *I* am'.

'Closure' is often assumed to be healing in emotional life. But, whatever the relationship between emotions and other forms of knowing, the premature closure of assumed knowledge may be anything but. We may indulge in such a fetish without understanding its possible consequences.

> Our knowledge will take its revenge on us, just as ignorance exacted its revenge during the Middle Ages.
>
> Karl Jaspers quoted in Sass (1992: 324)

Pessoa knew that there are "things of the soul and the consciousness that live in the interstices of knowledge" (2010: 125). Heaven forbid, though, that we fetishise ignorance in our retreat from the opposite c(o)urse. An endorsement of the possible potential in not-knowing is not a glorification of rampant ignorance. We may be guided by a natural balance: as the boundary of our knowledge increases so does its hinterland of not-knowing. The more we know, the more we have a sense of what we don't. That itself is a form of what Paul Pearsall calls 'open-ture'(2007: 3).

Self-identity involves self-grounding, a reliance on the security of an assumed selfhood which is both taken as known and serves as the arbiter of knowledge. But if humanity (human life) manifests as essentially interactive mystery/creativity – meaning that which cannot be programmed for production, but which must emerge in the moment – such a self-grounding must be relinquished for it will be a form of restrictive closure.

Nietzsche warned us of the god of grammar. What we reify we can readily deify – assume it as the supreme, primary reality. We can do that with ourselves. For the Buddhist, as we shall see, there is actually nothing to relinquish – in terms of assumed selfhood – other than our misplaced sense of reality. It can be useful to think of the self in this regard as more like a verb than a noun. This is one reason neurosis can be seen in Buddhist psychology as a kind of kōan. Kōans are riddling statements designed to loosen the stranglehold of conceptual knowledge (sometimes via exhaustion, sometimes via insight). The kōan is, in a sense, designed by the master as a meta-neurosis; for the question underlying all kōans is 'who is it that suffers?' "Bring me the self that would be liberated", one student was challenged; and he could not do so.

There is no enduring, secure ground. Nothing remains. Nothing is fixed. In every moment there is loss – that moment is gone. In every moment there is possibility – a new future opens up. Each moment is birth-and-death. The 'now' is the bittersweet cusp between the two. Life – experience – is always double-entry. We also look forwards; we also look backwards. The 'now' may have power, as Eckhart Tolle argues. But duration, temporality and situatedness have humanity in them, too.

We see what's there; we see what isn't there. Given the nature of our consciousness, we sometimes feel what isn't there as 'something', even if we're not sure quite what. Because our language is full of non-material abstractions, what is not substantially present can nevertheless have considerable valence.

Keats applauded Shakespeare's "negative capability" – an ease in doubt and mystery with no desire to reduce the texture of experience, to grasp prematurely at the securities of fact and reason. Those familiar with Zen will know Shunryu Suzuki's observation: "In the beginner's mind there are many possibilities. In the expert's mind there are few." (2010: 1). Winnicott urged that an analyst be able to tolerate not-knowing so that the "capacity to play", replacing the "epistemophilic instinct" (associated by him with Melanie Klein)[1], became a prime "criterion for health" (Phillips, 1988: 47). Casement, too, talks of a "creative tension" (1985: 5) between knowing and not-knowing and in turn quotes Bion's call for "a penetrating beam of darkness" (ibid: 225). Gestalt practitioners have their 'creative void', a space of creative potential. Given that therapists talk of bringing material to light, and seers of enlightenment, it is counterintuitive to promote 'darkness' as a virtue but the point is surely clear. Stars shine against darkness. Darkness allows light to show itself. Darkness, that is, and its cognate 'manifestations': not-knowing, absence and silence.

We need only note, though, how Keats's phrase has become so prevalent in therapeutic literature to see how quickly theory that sets out to denote a kind of receptivity and fluidity, can be assimilated into frameworks of thought and end up evoking the very kind of substantive presence it refutes. Therapeutically, theory is a way in, but not the way out. It can inform the practice, but not direct the outcome – though it may serve retrospectively as a lens for analysis and reflection. Loyalty is to the client, not the model.

---

[1] Winnicott was also aware of the potential reductiveness and intrusiveness of the analytic venture: "We can understand the hatred people have of psychoanalysis which has penetrated a long way into the human personality, and which provides a threat to the human individual in his need to be secretly isolated." (Phillips, 1988: 145, quoting Winnicott)

Hidebound conformity and gratuitous randomness are both to be avoided. Both the client and the therapist have their own inner recesses of not-knowing which should be honoured; and each is initially unknown to the other.

If counsellors sometimes hold on to theory to prop up their own identities as counsellors, it is not surprising how tightly clients can hold onto what appears to give them substance – however painful that is. I recall a young female client who came in and announced that she had a couple of issues she wanted help with. She was initially secretive about what they were. They were personal and intimate. I was intrigued and she seemed to enjoy the 'seductive' hide-and-seek element to our sessions. When she shared one of the things that was troubling her – and we had worked through it and some of the emotional energy seemed to have been dissipated – she switched her focus to the other one with some flourish and dismissed the first one we had looked at as being of little importance. Her issues, she seemed to believe, at some level, gave her her identity; but not only that – they made her interesting and gave her a certain mystique and allure. Of course, these issues and behaviours were within a context that was unique to her. I was interested in her problems; but I was equally interested in who she was behind them. In time, that person behind the problems, alive and spontaneous, began to emerge and – when she began to see that that person could be more interesting and engaging than her problems – *they* began to recede. For all sorts of reasons (often effectively drip-fed over a long period), many people either do not trust, or have lost contact with, who they are. That may sound as if it is contradicting my previous points about the fluidity and insubstantiality of self but it is not – because nothing arrests and rigidifies the self as much as neurosis. There is something about neurosis that almost always involves a kind of spinning on the spot – think of the issue-less energy aroused in anxiety, the inert ruminations of depression or the elastic tether that characterises obsession and compulsion.

Sharing the Light – and Darkness

The Italian philosopher Vico argued that, given the way we creatively engage with the world, as well as *a priori* (logical) and *a posteriori* (empirical) knowledge we need another category to understand human beings: that knowledge derived from 'reconstructive imagination'. Understanding involves 'entering into' (*entrare*) – that is, entering into a means of expression and participation that is not one's own. Isaiah Berlin, too, sees this as a new way of knowing: "knowledge indigenous to a way of life". We might further compare it to Wittgenstein's idea of 'forms of life' (Shotter, 1981: 267-271).[2] We can certainly see in it a precursor to the therapeutic emphases on empathy and the phenomenological experience of the client – how the world *appears* to him. If the client can explain and present his worldview to the therapist, he may well, during that process, clarify things to himself and, given the right conditions, move beyond preconceptions, self-concepts and 'scripts'.

It is for this reason, amongst others, that the therapist seeks to engage with the person rather than treat a diagnosis. How, after all, can one respect the client's life-world if one is already shoe-horning him into pre-existing categories? Therapy values boundaries, for sure, but that kind of premature constraint (or closure) will offer no transformative liberation.

> Darkness is your candle.
> Your boundaries are your quest.

So wrote Rumi. This, another image of light and dark, brings us back to, and partially illuminates, the by-now familiar murkiness. Darkness may, as suggested, yield light, and not-knowing clear the ground for knowing; but, it should be added, neither darkness nor not-knowing need be driven out completely. They need not be mere precursors to their elimination. That can be dangerous: our rational wisdom itself should alert us to our enduring shadow side and our humility protect us from the sometime absence of our wisdom. We all, too, including me in this essay, have to engage with the slipperiness of language and the limits of thought. There is no firm ground on which to stand. So, strange to say, I hope, and trust, that my own ignorance, where appropriate, shines through. Premature and false claims to knowledge are often pre-emptive strikes against doubt, mystery, complexity and humanity.

The *Via Negativa* Analogy

Via negativa speaks of what isn't there, what isn't the case – and thereby makes its case.

It is most widely used in the field of mysticism where, to borrow an idea from Meister Eckhart, if one seeks (and speaks of) ways to God, one finds only *ways*, not God. In mysticism – where it is sometimes termed apophasis or negative theology – it is basically an ironic denial of God; ironic because

---

[2] Shotter relies heavily on Isaiah Berlin's analysis (1976: xvi-xix).

it denies God to emphasise His status: language cannot take the measure of Him. Because God (or any ultimate reality) is a "superabundance of meaning", (McIntosh, 1998: 123) God can outstrip whatever we can say about Him. By saying, therefore, what He is *not*, and exhausting knowable and speakable possibilities, we clear a space, as it were, in which He might be encountered in his reality without the limitations that our language implicitly sets on Him. The paradox, of course, is that we do this using language and so are caught in the same trap – just, perhaps, on the reverse, conscious side of it.

The ideas of clearing a space and opening up unknown possibilities would seem to be transferable to the situation, and process, of therapy. They can also apply to our attempts to denote linguistically what happens in the therapy session – attempts which never seem to quite coincide with the experiential reality – and to the client's own process and progress. These limitations might be seen as concentric rings coming to the sharpest focus on the client. There is a somewhat impenetrable and inexpressible reality at the centre of the encounter. (This impenetrability may extend to the level of inner realisation let alone mere denotation. If we are, as we may be, fundamentally non-coincident with ourselves, can we *ever* achieve secure self-knowledge – one of the holy grails of much therapy and spiritual practice? Can we even decisively embrace/accept our constitutive eccentricity?)

It may be that "no desire is more natural than the desire for knowledge" – as Montaigne wrote as the first sentence of *On Experience*, quoting the first sentence of Aristotle's *Metaphysics*. But is this desire, in fact, natural; or is it a cultural bias? Do we fetishise knowledge because it is assumed to bring security, a security we desire, for sure, because we do not wish to face the inevitable insecurity of life? The value, though, of security depends on what one is secure in. It is perhaps *insecurity*, in this regard, that those who have mastered the art of living are best at accepting. Perhaps such people, too, rely more on knowledge by acquaintance rather than an abstract, discursive and speculative knowledge 'about' – one that can be passed on somehow without having been earned and tested experientially. The latter can – especially if it anticipates the nature of something – even act as a barrier against it.

Returning to therapy, if the client had full knowledge – of who and where he was, where he wanted to go and how to get there – he might well not have needed to see a therapist in the first place. The client tends to want to escape certain feelings; the therapist to facilitate his reconnection to, and acceptance of, them. The client may indeed, initially, be seeking premature certainty and closure, seeking to follow his own path of imposition; but, in the words of Wallace Stevens, "to impose is not / To discover". In the *Genjo Kōan*, Dōgen suggests that the 'aim' of practice is to be able to sit without purpose; but most of us would have to sit for a very long time until we could do that. Partly for these reasons, therapy often proceeds by a kind of deconstruction.[3] The client grows into the gaps in his idea of himself.

> *I described O as being racked with anxiety. The word is fitting. She is on a Procrustean bed of self-censorship, attempting to shape the organismic flow of her experience to preconceived notions of what is acceptable and what is not. I listen to her non-judgementally, prompting her to go wider and deeper than her current preoccupation with her symptoms prompts her.*

The emphasis in some therapy and much meditative practice is to attend, to observe and to 'sit with' – without judgement or seeking to control (be that drawing something near or pushing it away). It is about accepting and embracing the uninterrupted flow of sensation without habitual, especially compulsive, reaction patterns. In such a state, we feel ourselves as much told as teller. We flicker in and as the flame between seer and seen.

For all their differences – and it is not my intention to deny them (just because the unknown may be infinite does not necessarily make it religious) – both mystical contemplation and therapy often seem to be arts of subtraction, of letting go. The client has – consciously or unconsciously – adopted various forms of defensive behaviour and 'symptoms' which serve(d) some purpose, but which are no longer skilful and productive ways of living. Furthermore, the therapist agrees in part to subordinate his own process, and certainly any excessive self-interest, in the interests of the client.

We might characterise a 'typical' progress, if there is such a thing, in therapy as a movement from unskilful living, through a transitional phase in which the client relinquishes certain of these behaviours and tendencies, to a readiness to go back to the world and live better. It is with that middle phase – one of transition, for sure, but also of suspension of assumed

---

[3] I am perhaps not using this term in its strictest philosophical sense although there are counterparts to many of the points I am making in modern theory. Deleuze, for example, calls for a "continuous recommencement" to replace any claims to finality of knowledge. See Gutting (2001: 38).

knowledge, security and familiarity, a liminal region, Winnicott's playful, potential space (1971) – that *via negativa* might most readily be compared. In fact, the language of commentary can be startlingly similar. In mystical theology, the place of God (i.e. any attempt at a conceptual representation) is a "place that is not-a-place", a "flickering", an otherness that "disturbs all attempts to establish either full presence or full absence" (Turner & Davies, 2001: 40-41). Describing the role of the therapist, and echoing Winnicott, Casement similarly notes that:

> the therapist's presence therefore has to remain a transitional or potential presence (like that of a mother who is non-intrusively present with her playing child). The therapist can then be invoked by the patient as a presence, or can be used by the patient as an absence. (1985: 30)

Much literature on counselling values the solid, grounded presence of the therapist; but that presence is of a particular kind. It combines a focus and intensity vis-à-vis the client and also a being-present to whatever emerges. It is a quality of being. Whatever the theoretical stance of the therapist, the containment this presence offers comes from the model he himself embodies – one of receptive fluidity: he manifests not a bracing against experience but an openness to it. The life-world contains "open, endless horizons of things unknown" (Husserl, 1970: 149). This is an openness to possibility rather than a retreat into fixity and identity. The problems that clients bring to therapy often involve a closed-off-ness. We should do all we can to ensure that the 'answers' they find with us do not do the same. That would be only the most superficial and unhelpful type of transformation.

The Human Dimension

Conversely, all this talk of metaphysics and negativity need not detract from the simple power of the human encounter. I remember well the poignancy of the moment a highly intellectual client had rehearsed his usual approach to the distress in his life, only to conclude with a heartfelt "I don't know where I'm going with this". With a tone, timing and genuineness that owed at least as much to a basic humanity as any formal training, I simply replied, half-smiling, "Me neither". Something shifted in that moment. I had not sought to rescue him or reassure him. I had heard and understood (and he had heard and understood my understanding) his struggle to accept that his normal frameworks of encounter with his challenges were not the life raft he thought they were but were instead a barrier to the currents of experience that might have moved him onwards, out of his cognitive whirlpool. He wished to move forward but had pinned himself in concepts and the past, unavailable to genuine encounter with self, life or other. Sometimes, as the popular analogy puts it, we have to lose sight of the shore to reach new lands.

This process, and the one that Casement describes, might be termed natal or eventive. It is irreducible to the language of pre-existing entities. This non-essential nature of selfhood – nothing fixed, substantial, intrinsic, eternal or even consistent – can be forbidding; not least when the word used to denote it, *sunyata*, is often translated as 'emptiness'. Others, including Watson (2002) have suggested that 'openness' might better evoke its qualities. As Welwood writes:

> Looking within, you may find no single thing to grasp onto, nothing that easily fits into a conceptual box. [...] To tap the healing power within us, we first have to let ourselves *not know*, so that we can make contact with the fresh, living texture of our experience, beyond all our familiar thoughts. (2000: 142)

Nietzsche, it seems, would concur:

> I mistrust all systematizers and avoid them. The will to a system is a lack of integrity. (1990: I, 26)

If I can, over a number of sessions, accept all that O shows me of herself (including her resistance to certain aspects of herself), in time she may do likewise. She may even come to accept those elements of herself that she chooses to keep secret from me. That is fine. I am not an inquisitor.

Mindfulness

The question of mindfulness (such a contemporary buzzword) cannot be addressed fully here but is certainly relevant. With wise caveats in mind – namely: that what one is mindful *of* is crucially important; and that mindfulness can readily and insidiously degenerate into self-indulgence, dissociation or mere vagueness – what I am endorsing here, an openness to experience without a wish to marshal it into preconceived categories, would indeed coincide with at least some definitions of mindfulness. This may, in a sense, be an affirmation of authentic 'otherness' in oneself as therapist, as well as in the client. It is the human burden to negotiate with the vital and emergent energies of life; but it is not our duty to tame the life out of them.

Mindfulness is an openness to the ever-changing texture of life. Structures – of whatever type – are provisional, heuristic, there potentially to move us beyond structures. In mindfulness, we "perceive the unbridgeable gap between life as it is and our *ideas* about it". Ideas are themselves structures – useful in helping us organise and communicate experience but "not knowing [may be] valuable because it may not only enable therapy but it is also ultimately the truth of the matter" (Fulton, 2005: 71).

Whether or not one uses the *language* of mindfulness, one can adopt a similar attitude or orientation: "I learnt to be true to what emerges in sessions with the client without trying to fit it into pre-established frames of reference." These are the words of Emmy Van Deurzen, an existential practitioner. She goes on:

> I now look forward to moments of being stuck temporarily, having understood that they signify the new opportunities to rediscover my own ignorance and the endless variations of human experience. (1992: 40)

One is not insistent on acquiring an instrumental knowledge, one that can be implemented scientifically. The widespread appeal of that kind of knowledge should by now be clear. In Hawking's words: "If you understand how the universe operates, you control it, in a way" (2013). A hunger for control is seductive on two levels: we are vulnerable and we are greedy. But neither the deep wellsprings, nor the deep conditions, of life are amenable to it. It is in this sense, amongst others, that:

> Self, it turns out, is a metaphor for a process we do not understand, a metaphor for that which *knows*. The insight practices reveal that such a metaphor is unnecessary, even disruptive. It is enough, these practices reveal, to open to the ongoing process of knowing without imputing some*one* behind it all. (Epstein, 1995: 155)

That notional someone is the executive ego, seeking influence and security; ego as both producer and product of such inclinations. Awareness, with practice, can gain insight into the insubstantial shadow play that is its real nature:

> Through sharpening our mindfulness, we start to catch ourselves in the act of constructing stories and can see them as the fabrications they are. We start to see how we are

> continually trying to draw conclusions about who we are, what we are doing, and what will happen next. (Welwood, 2000: 177)

From Freud to contemporary practitioners, many therapists have endorsed a non-judgemental, quasi-meditative openness to experience, inside and outside the therapy session.

The *via negativa* of mystical theology has also been characterised as an "openness of meaning" (Turner & Davies, 2002: 40). To a large degree this attitude, on the one hand, and self-concepts and tightly held personal narratives, on the other, are mutually exclusive. We exist not only in but *as* the flicker of signification. The accent moves, then, from preconceived and protected identity to engagement, interaction and other-connectedness. This is consistent, too, with the narrative therapy of Michael White and David Epston. A tenet of that model is 'the person is not the problem'. 'Thin' (i.e. negative and limiting) narratives – to use their terms – need to be jettisoned. (Whether one need replace them with 'thicker' ones, as they suggest, is debatable.) Many people, perhaps all – given that we *are* reflective creatures with an awareness of time – do see their lives as, and through, stories, so an ability to adapt and extemporise our story-making would certainly retain some of the potential for spontaneous and authentic response that *via negativa* seeks to safeguard (Loy, 2010).

The Interpreted World, Fantasy and Abstraction

As far as we can tell, the way human beings experience the world is unique – and part of our uniqueness is that we reflect on how we experience the world. On a sensory level, we only see one aspect of an object because our senses cannot capture it all simultaneously; but we trust that the world that is not there in our immediate view *is* still there. Knowledge of this type, "unlike sentience, is unique to humans" (Tallis, 2012: 186). Unlike even chimpanzees, our closest cousins, we have a sense of there being "continuous, relatively stable, objects existing independently of our sense experiences, with an intrinsic nature hidden from us" (ibid). Chimpanzees, by contrast, are instinct-led within immediate experience. Our thought processes can, therefore, keep in our awareness material objects (whose empirical reality we *could* check) and – perhaps building on this ability, and given our gift for abstraction and the layers and levels of our feeling-world and imaginations – we also have an apparently inexhaustible inner life of meaning, memory, image and fantasy through which we live. This is one of the reasons why our attempts to pin things down with language always risk putting a straitjacket on that very vitality that distinguishes us. Definition is so often restriction. We tie our own hands and minds and hearts. If therapists are not to get trapped in their own models, ideas and theoretical grids, they have to keep 'soft eyes' – an ability to see what is there rather than looking for what may not be. Looking *for* can even sometimes equate to looking through. And no client wants the sense of having been seen through (or 'shrunk'). "Theory is good, but it doesn't prevent things from existing", as Jean-Martin Charcot is alleged to have said.

The anthropological wing of religious studies also alerts us to something else that has equal relevance in the therapeutic encounter: namely, the difference between the esoteric and the exoteric, the emic and the etic, the immediate and the culturally mediated – the former in each case suggesting that which can only be fully grasped from the inside, from the phenomenological heart of the experience (which returns us to Vico's ideas outlined above). In the world of created meaning, objectivity can only go so far. We can seek to look at ourselves (as we do others) in the third person;[4] but we experience the world most acutely from the first person, however contextually dependent that may be. We may wish – for reasons touched on above – to secure ourselves in the rational, objectifying, executive centre of our minds, to see through analytical sights, but other dimensions of ourselves make their own calls on us, too. Our hearts, for one; and our bodies, for, as Larkin wrote, "our flesh / Surrounds us with its own decisions". Our bodies, as mindfulness practice reminds us, are in constant flux and our bodies are less amenable, for that reason, to the static ideas that our conceptual minds seek to impose for control and security.

Theories and Models

It is true that our 'problems' – those things that bring us to therapy – are caused and held in place by conditions. The conditions of the therapy situation – which provides a structure that ultimately mitigates stricture –

[4] Do we *always* do that, in fact, as soon as we *talk* from the first person perspective because of the distancing effect of language? And, furthermore, if I refer to myself (as I am now) at one remove, I still assume that that objective self has a first person. So, first becomes third, and third becomes first, each containing or switching to the other in infinite regress.

offer a space for exploration. It is not paradoxical to say, therefore, that the model of therapy should be envisioned as a window rather than a picture. It is an operative framework that permits (like a window) its own casting-aside as opening occurs. It is, after all, not the therapist's role to promote an agenda or convince the client of the efficacy of his particular model.

It is precisely because, as I would argue, therapy seeks – if, by this argument, it can be said to seek anything – to engender such a state of openness to experience, that it can be very challenging to say precisely what it does involve. But, if we accept that perception is often characterised by framing, bias and filters, then we return to the idea that therapy is often – like sculpture – a process or art of removal. But the final figure in therapy is unknown. Trying to describe in advance what will be uncovered by un-asking and unmasking risks setting up more of the kind of preconception and instrumental directedness that one is moving beyond. As in mystical theory, deconditioning always risks a *re*conditioning; but vitality and creativity make, find and observe, in the unfolding moment.

In this light we might ask an even more provocative question: namely, are all therapeutic models and techniques merely *pretexts* – ones that allow clients to do something (almost *any*thing) while they learn how to be and how to relate, with the models and techniques themselves only provisionally necessary to that process? The techniques might also be there to satisfy the *therapist* that he is doing something constructive, as Yalom suggested. It certainly seems that the quality of the encounter and the spirit, energy, ethos and relatedness in which the therapy happens are of more crucial importance than the explicit model or method. Loy (1987) argues that Derrida ultimately fails in his deconstructive project because he demands to remain present (if only linguistically)[5] as the arbiter of his own arguments. One might argue that the good therapist is characterised by his willingness to do exactly the opposite.

For Morotomi (cited in Thorne, 2002: 50), the person-centred encounter (and, we might argue, any genuinely therapeutic encounter) allows the client to enter a "vacuum" of aloneness in which all psycho-emotional disturbances are relinquished ('held' by the therapist in fact) – so the client can pursue his "inward journey". One might also think again of the 'creative void' of Gestalt in this regard. Because of its emphasis on non-attachment, it is very easy to misconstrue Buddhist psychology as an endorsement of

---

[5] Derrida refutes immediate presence-to-self but it is interesting to consider whether our inner talk is itself a way of seeking to affirm ourselves to ourselves.

detachment. Nothing could be further from the truth. What it seeks to see through is reactive conditioning and compulsion – to a more complete engagement with the world. This is in contrast to a withdrawn protection of self as a narcissistic centre, and life as an aggregation of habit. One gains an insight into how an illusory and defensive self colours experience. One sees more fully, more openly, by seeing into the contamination generated by (and as) this reified selfhood.

While *via negativa* in theology is ironic (God denied, the better to affirm Him); in therapy it is not. That is, of course, the crucial difference. In therapy the negation of elements is not done to bolster a substantial, core reality; quite the opposite, in fact. It is to allow a deeper, more skilful engagement with life. But, if our rational explanations of the process fail us, that does not necessarily invite the irrational. It might merely point to the arational elements of existence and those that resist reductive verbal transcription. Therapy occurs via many channels, not just the verbal and cognitive. So, if set patterns dissolve, one is not necessarily led to regressive dependency or mystical vortex. As we saw, there may be a period when the therapist needs to 'hold' the client with care until character realignments develop – but the client will emerge to more abundant living. It is the unhelpful defences, distortions and delusions that one works through; and whether or not one can *denote* a more fruitful 'reality' in advance does not affect that process. One develops the faith to doubt – where faith is contrasted with a preconceived certainty.

Whatever the model of therapy, the therapist, then, tends to put in place the conditions, and sometimes employ the techniques, which challenge self-concept, excessive rationalisation, generalisations and all manner of other defences – defences that developed to deal with the existential and emotional challenges of life but which have become an outdated encumbrance to living. The ego, after all, as we have seen, likes to think of itself as separate and in control. As Frances Vaughan notes:

> Those experiences that it cannot control, it resists. Just as the normal developmental transition from dependence to independence is experienced as frightening and difficult at times, the transition from independence to interdependence can also seem threatening. Nonetheless it is essential to healing and wholeness." (1986: 181)

After several sessions together, O reports feeling more relaxed and confident. I have not cured her. I have no secret knowledge or power.

> *If I have anything, it is a way of being with her (and with myself). I could not explain with any certainty how and why O's symptoms have abated – though I am interested. O is not interested in the theory of it all. She is not a psychologist. I may now describe her as being more fully integrated, less repressed, more self-actualised, less in thrall to ideas about herself and how she should be – her self-stories. It doesn't alter the reality – which is that I didn't know we would end up here, I'm not sure how we got here and I'm not even sure where 'here' is. Theoretical maps might speculate on the route we have taken but they could not in themselves have led us here.*

It is very easy to think of transpersonal psychology as quasi-religious or – that most nebulous of nebulous words – spiritual; but, in Vaughan's description, and in terms of Buddhist thinking, it need mean no more than freedom from the prison of egoic selfhood. One does not lose *sense* of self or sense of subject(ivity); nor does one lose ego-*functions*. It is simply that one is not falsely identified with them and held in their grip. We stop putting the cart before the horse, blocking our way forward.

One *can* go further down the religious road. Thorne does explicitly compare the nondual element of the therapeutic encounter with Zen training, Christian mysticism and universal love. Whether or not we are comfortable with such overt and literal comparisons, many therapists would probably accept some kind of "relational depth" (Thorne, 2002: 51) as being central to successful work, though that term is itself highly contentious. We *need* not, though, define what the transegoic 'something larger' is or where it is located. Thorne, and Rogers himself, might also be criticised for a naïve and overoptimistic view of human nature (not least because an increased, more diffuse awareness may well invite awareness of shadow material) but, if the awareness is more conscious and less reactive, it should also diminish any 'acting out' and allow for more skilful responsiveness and more complete integration.

I am not yet a highly experienced therapist; so I make my next point with due deference to those who are. Human beings are very responsive to patterns: we make them and we are quick to spot them. When one has been seeing clients year after year it must be very easy to pick up on various indicators and to 'type' clients – to think we 'know' them in this limited, labelling way. Perhaps the inexperienced therapist is less likely to fall prey to this particular tendency. The problem with it should be clear. It risks seeing the constellation of symptoms and missing the person. It is incumbent on the therapist – even the most empathic one – not to entirely share the client's preoccupation with the overwhelming impact of the presenting issue. The 'problem' is not the client – even though it may have served some purpose for him to believe that. So the skilled therapist does not believe that the client – let alone a textbook – is telling the whole possible story. This is suspicion of the most benevolent kind. There are other ways of seeing, saying, feeling, doing and being. That is the faith in possibility that the therapist embodies and upholds. The client can come to know more; but one dimension of that increased knowledge might be an awareness that there are certain things that he *cannot* know and cannot control.

As John Welwood argues, when therapists are interested in what they do not know about their clients (often what the client does not yet consciously know about himself; and what he may never know) he is less likely to be manipulative and egotistical himself; and more likely to be an authentic fellow-traveller into mystery and potential. This tends to be the reality of the process of therapy, I would suggest, whatever model it uses to theorise the details to its workings. Whether one characterises this as primarily psychotherapeutic or 'spiritual' is, I would argue, of secondary importance. Suffice it to say, it is concerned with growth and fulfilment. The known that it works from is an openness to the unknown.

O is now out in the world and I know nothing of her progress. We explored her values, her ideas about herself, her way of relating – to herself and others. We sat with feelings she may formerly have chosen to deny or seek escape from. I assume she has not given up her preference for pleasurable feelings over painful ones; but I hope she has more understanding of how her attempts to guarantee the former or deal with the latter may have been counter-productive. She can still choose her path in life but may not insist on constant control, on being able to make her life-world – and the others, people and situations that constitute it – match her template, join her on her Procrustean bed. For I trust she now knows that even when she sought that control, it did not happen; often, because she sought it. She lives with a new quality of being rather than a set of conditions to which life must conform. If she is living well, and I hope and trust she is, she too will know that openness to the unknown.

References

Berlin, I. (1976) *Vico and Herder*, Hogarth Press

Casement, R. (1985) *On Learning from the Patient*, Tavistock

Epstein, M. (1995) *Thoughts Without a Thinker*, Basic Books

Fulton, P. R. (2005) 'Mindfulness as Clinical Training' in Germer, C.K., Siegel, R.D. & Fulton, P.R. (eds.) *Mindfulness and Psychotherapy*, Guilford Press

Gutting, G. (2001) *Thinking the Impossible*, Oxford University Press

Hawking, S. (2013) *My Brief History: A Memoir*, Bantam

Husserl, E. (1970) *The Crisis of European Sciences and Transcendental Phenomenology*, Northwestern University Press

Loy, D. (1987) 'The *Clôture* of Deconstruction: A Mahayana Critique of Derrida', *International Philosophical Quarterly*, Vol XXVII, No 1, Issue 105, March 1987

____ (2010), *The World is Made of Stories*, Wisdom Publications

McIntosh, M. A. (1998) *Mystical Theology*, Blackwell

Nietzsche, F. (1990) *Twilight of the Idols and the Anti-Christ*, Penguin Classics

Pearsall, P. (2007) *Awe*, Health Communications

Pessoa, F. (2010) *Book of Disquiet*, Profile Books

Phillips, A. (1988) *Winnicott*, Fontana

Sass, L. (1992) *Madness and Modernism*, Basic Books

Shotter, J. (1981) 'Vico, Moral Worlds, Accountability and Personhood', in Heelas, P & Lock, A. (eds.) *Indigenous Psychologies - The Anthropology of the Self*, Academic Press

Suzuki, S. (2010) *Zen Mind, Beginner's Mind*, Shambhala,

Tallis, R. (2012) *In Defence of Wonder*, Acumen

Thorne, B. (2002) *The Mystical Power of Person-Centred Therapy*, Whurr

Turner, D. & Davies, O. eds. (2001) *Silence and the Word*, Cambridge University Press

Van Deurzen, E. (1992) 'Chapter 3' in Dryden, W. (ed.) *Hard-Earned Lessons from Counselling in Action*, Sage Publications

Vaughan, F. (1986) *The Inward Arc*, Shambhala

Watson, G. (2002) *The Resonance of Emptiness*, Routledge

Welwood, J (2000) *Toward a Psychology of Awakening*, Shambhala

Winnicott, D. W. (1971) *Playing and Reality*, Tavistock

Planting an Oak in a Flowerpot

Manu Bazzano

'Knowing' is a fetish. It gives us brief comfort against life's inherent uncertainty. Socratic 'not-knowing' is another, 'softer' kind of fetish, at times adopted by psychotherapists and Dharma practitioners alike to heighten our humanistic and religious credentials. This chapter explores – via a case study, a reading of Dōgen's notion of pilgrimage (*hansan*), and elements of Emily Brontë's novel *Wuthering Heights* – a form of 'not-knowing' that points towards the unknowable.

Several traditions speak of the unknowable, using different names: the organism, the unconscious, the ultimate. By resisting a sectarian compulsion to reify any of these notions and claim direct and exclusive access to them, we may avoid the literalism of religion. By exploring them freely, we may also avoid the secularist fallacy of explaining the world away and absurdly attempting, as Heathcliff says in *Wuthering Heights*, to 'plant an oak in a flowerpot'.

The White Room (Jenny's dream)

I am a guest in Tony's house, but the house looks bigger and with one or two extra floors at the top. Tony's entire extended family is here. His wife, a banker, talks animatedly on her mobile in French, looking busy and important. I'm shown a small, pleasant room, with a futon on the floor: I'm going to sleep here during my weekend visit. I understand why I'm here: I've been given (implicitly) an important task. I must enter a room haunted by Tony's brother, who died a while ago. I must speak to the ghost and set him free. The room is white and utterly empty. To enter, I must go through two separate doors with a space in the middle. When I get there, I feel an agonising cold all over me; I am gripped by terror. Even so, I want to keep on, perform my task and prove my spiritual prowess to myself and Tony. But the cold is too intense and the spectral presence – now ever so tangible, ominous – overpowers me. I rush out to my room, where I collapse on the mattress, weeping.

A moment later, Tony comes in and lies next to me; he would like to comfort me but doesn't know how to. He just can't understand my pain. We are both half naked. I worry what his wife and the rest of the family may think, seeing us lying there. I am nervous they will find out about our affair. Tony's two brothers come in, followed by his sister. Lunch is ready and we are all expected downstairs.

I have a revelation: I see how Tony wants me there so that things will precipitate, come to a head, and find a dramatic resolution without him having to do a thing. With his family finally learning about the affair, everything will irremediably change for the better. My presence acts as a catalyst. Exhausted as well as upset by this insight, I want to leave but I can't move. I pause for a few minutes. Then I get up and take a long breath. I gather all my courage and run out of the door.

Outside it's already dark. Fear has left me and I walk lightly, happy and unnoticed among the anonymous passers-by. Climbing up the granite steps from a familiar square, I wonder what has changed: 'I never ever believed in ghosts' – I say quietly to myself – 'but now I'm not so sure'.

That night Jenny woke up sweating and in her very bones she felt the dream carried an important message. She told me so two days later at one of her weekly sessions. The dream also marked a shift in therapy. She had been Tony's lover for the past six months – both of them married, but seeking something more; both managing to keep it going somehow, in spite of the difficulties: the convoluted logistics, but also the very palpable remorse that she (more than he) felt, carrying the burden, as she put it, for both. She knew her dream marked something momentous, but what? "To get out, perhaps?" – I suggested. It was obvious to me, but made a point to sound tentative. "Sure ... maybe", she said, "but there is something else here, hard to grasp; I want to know more, I want to understand." For my part, I couldn't quite bracket my conviction that a married woman having an affair with a married man wasn't such a smart idea and that there would be misery for all concerned. I did try of course the *epoché* thing, the phenomenological reduction, or suspension of judgement. I tried to be the Merleau-Pontian perpetual beginner, something I advocate in lectures and papers. But didn't the great Maurice say that it is precisely by attempting to practise it that the suspension is shown as an impossible task?

Whatever the case may be, the one thing that persisted was the image of that white room, so vividly rendered by Jenny, as well as the strangely concrete, semi-corporeal presence of the ghost. Jenny never actually saw the ghost in her dream, but his presence was pervasive. The palpitations and the cold sweat had been real enough. She conveyed them so directly that I had also felt the icy shiver. Did the ghost *stand for* something, I wondered sheepishly (guiltily even, for how can a self-confessed phenomenologist ever be lured by the siren of symbolism and symbolic interpretation?). I, of course, believe that dream phenomena are not to be read as hieroglyphs, whose true meaning patiently awaits my allegedly expert decoding, or as symbols replacing the barren existence of things and people, but ought to be discerned instead as direct, thoroughly demystified and very real experience.

Both Jenny and I felt stuck, in spite of two sessions dedicated to being with the dream and staying open to its meaning.

An Oak in a Flowerpot

Emily was the most philosophically-minded among the Brontë children, and her *Wuthering Heights* "goes straight to the heart of the question of agency and freedom" (Nussbaum, 2011: 607). Way beyond the cliché that anaesthetises it as Gothic literary entertainment, the novel remains positively disturbing in its portrayal of possibilities outside the static view of final causes found in Christian and moral love. The love between Heathcliff and Catherine soars above the static goal-oriented ethos of religiosity, affirming the greater import of human agency and freedom over the domesticated effusions given by Linton, whom Catherine ends up marrying: a man whose attempts at dealing with the daimon of love are akin to planting an oak in a flowerpot.

> The world, the suggestion is, will always remain a Hell if we are allowed to aim at redemption from it, rather than at the amelioration of life within it, and led to anticipate the end of striving, rather than to respect the dignity of the striving itself. (ibid: 607)

This is not the place to elaborate on ethics and its relation to aesthetics and to muse whether in fact seeing the former as a branch of the latter might help wrangle it from the religious stronghold (as well as the secular/utilitarian one) in which it remains caught (Bazzano, 2012). But it might be useful to register that the passional and passionate *event* called 'Heathcliff and Catherine' points at an aesthetics – hence is 'para-ethical' (Surin, 2011):

> There is no schema of evaluation (the requisite hallmark of ethics) within which the event of 'Heathcliff and Catherine' can be contained in order to make it explicable and seemingly rational. (ibid: 150)

A mediocre commentator will appreciate the splendour and 'entertainment value' of this tragic love. In the same way perhaps the average therapist will welcome the usefulness of the clinical material his client's upheavals represent in fostering an existing – and anodyne – 'body of knowledge'.

Love at Last Sight

'A married woman having an affair with a married man isn't a smart idea'. This thought, lodged in the back of my mind unchecked (let alone 'bracketed') was also, as it turned out, Jenny's own thought. One bright December morning, a week after her dream, she decided to end it with Tony. She had met him the previous day in a café and asked him out of the blue what it'd be like for him if one day it were to end, and he responded, rather plainly she thought, "Well, you know, I'd be sad". She didn't want to wait until she could meet him face to face so she phoned, and was glad to get his voicemail. Her message was to the point, but not unkind.

Only later, Jenny told me, she understood what that strange phrase meant, the one she had found in Walter Benjamin's writings: "love at last sight". She was "all jumbled emotion" and understood that it didn't matter that it was secret and short-lived and doomed to failure. For one thing, the pain made it holy. Its fleetingness did not in any way denigrate it. Listening to her, I felt at a loss. I couldn't think straight. Only now, with hindsight, I can begin to put into words the dim, conflicting thoughts and feelings I had at the time.

Can I, as a therapist, suspend my moral judgement on what is right and wrong? The love Tony and Jenny have for each other (I say 'have' in the present because they got together a month later) – however complicated and potentially disruptive – burns in the purity of its flame. Yes, of course it goes against 'conscience'. Of course erotic passion is the meeting point of the *unknown* and the *uncommitted.* I know all that. But what do we find at the opposite pole if not the idealisation of love and the denial of the erotic? And the sanctification of domestic boredom and routine, the altar on which many of us sacrifice our *jouissance* – a notion not only virtually untranslatable in contemporary English, but unfathomable in our current cultural climate. Unless, of course, psychotherapy is the last bastion of bourgeois morality and our task as practitioners is to educate the wayward pilgrims to the rightful path. But what is the rightful path? And what do I really know of the mysterious ways in which love operates?

I conveyed my hopelessness to Jenny and suggested we go back to square one. I did not openly admit my disapproval of her affair, or the obscure, irrational jealousy I had felt. Yes, I forgot to mention it: before meeting Tony, she had fallen in love with me. Textbook transference, of course: sensitive, good-looking, intelligent client who did not experience the same level of intimacy before inevitably falls for her therapist who hides behind the screen of clinical jargon and knowing; who hides behind the screen of Socratic/Platonic not-knowing; who cannot admit to himself (and his supervisor) how flattered he feels, how galvanised that someone finds *him* (with his little life of boring academic chores, average client work and serialised American dramas from Lovefilm as almost his sole source of amusement) fascinating! Who forgets Freud's self-deprecating witticism: nothing to do with his 'irresistible charm'.

Never mind. I more or less expertly help unravel and bypass the sticky phase of our therapeutic work by focusing on the task at hand: her process, her 'growth' (how I hate that word, as if people were vegetables!), her return to a 'healthier' state, away from flirtations, vagaries and infatuations. The thing is, though, I am not so certain any more – of what I am as a therapist, of what therapy is supposed to do. Perhaps someone will tell me. Perhaps someone will *clarify* it for me. Even though "to suppose that clarity proves anything about truth is perfect childishness" (Nietzsche, 1968: 538). Even though I can't help feeling that not-knowing (or the askesis of at-*tempt*-ing, giving in to the *tempt*-ation of not-knowing) momentarily exempts me from the obligation to join the psychotherapeutic, philosophical and religious choir that compels us all to cry in unison for order out of chaos, for implausible 'facts' against our endless and necessary mediations, for 'evidence' and, finally, for *truth as conformity*, i.e. the preservation of a set of historical prejudices to which we subscribe. Against this self-satisfied and self-created 'world', abnormality, distress and even abjection begin to take on distinctly *soulful* traits.

Learning or Being Affected

I am personally aware of two kinds of not-knowing – one stemming from Socratic/Platonic philosophy and one from the Zen tradition.

Socratic not-knowing – a welcome change from scientistic ambitions of all-conquering knowledge – is by far the more influential of the two and appears to overtly and covertly inform attempts within the metaphysical and rationalist tradition to curb our Promethean lust for subjugating and explaining away what surpasses limited human understanding.

This style of not-knowing has gained currency within some therapeutic orientations alongside Socratic questioning (built on Socrates's style of dialogue). Based on an understanding of learning as maieutics, i.e. midwifery, this notion is ingrained in the fabric of our thinking: the word *education* comes from the Latin *educere,* to draw out. According to this paradigm, the expert therapist/philosopher/educator draws out and brings to light, through skilled questioning at the edge of awareness, the jumbled fragments of the client's dormant wisdom. Expertise, far from being a mark of authority, is employed in the service of the client's well-being and self-determination. This model relies on a Platonic view of the human soul and on a 'classical', pre-phenomenological view of *psyche* as an apparatus separate from the world rather than embedded within it. There is, however, another perspective, according to which education is "no longer [understood] as extracting pre-existent knowledge and wisdom but instead as the product of an encounter with otherness" (Bazzano, 2012: 6). Championed and beautifully argued by Levinas (1961), this view has gained currency in recent philosophical discourse giving birth to a 'radical ethics of alterity' (Critchley, 2007; Agamben, 1998; Butler, 2004; Derrida, 2001; Bazzano, 2012) that did not simply rest on Levinas's valuable insights but has gone well beyond its limitations.

According to what it is still a work-in-progress model, learning occurs when we take more fully into account exteriority. 'Education' then comes to mean being deeply 'affected' and impacted by the presence of the other. I have sketched this idea in the first chapter of a recent book (Bazzano, 2012), highlighting the profound link between identity and otherness. Our identity is constructed against otherness. One could say that there is no such thing as interiority, for a thorough examination of the nature of the self reveals its non-substantiality as well as its ineffability. When we look closely, we do not find a thing we can call the self, an entity distinct from phenomena. Consciousness itself emerges from phenomena. The notion I have of myself is another phenomenon just like the traffic noise or the muffled sound of rain on this cold winter day. I simply cannot know myself as a solid and separate entity. This 'I' too belongs to exteriority. I am external to myself, unknowable to myself; a stranger to myself. This I itself belongs to otherness. "*Je est un autre*" (I is another), Rimbaud's famous phrase, is open to several meanings. Identity begins to falter as my observation becomes more precise.

A perspective rooted in otherness overturns the Platonic idea of maieutics and the very meaning of experience. The process of education is then no longer seen as extracting pre-existent knowledge and wisdom but instead as the product of a genuine encounter with otherness.

Conversely, Socrates's 'I know only that I do not know 'is essentially a dialectical trick, a way to pre-empt the interlocutor's potential criticism by admitting one's ignorance from the start. It also betrays reverence for knowledge itself, conspicuous by its very denial. This sort of 'not-knowing', dominant in Western thought, is a form of rational and dialectical sophism which betrays false modesty.

I Don't Know Nothing

The other type of not-knowing can be illustrated by the following Zen kōan:

> Dizang asked Fayan: "Where are you going?"
>
> Fayan said: "Around on a pilgrimage"
>
> Dizang said: "What is the purpose of pilgrimage?"
>
> Fayan said: "I don't know".
>
> Dizang said: "Not knowing is nearest". (Cleary, 1990: 86)

'Not knowing is nearest': one arrives at this kind of not-knowing having travelled far and wide, having left no stone unturned. It is a profound admission of defeat – a defeat which might well be our only hope for it preludes the abdication of the notion of a Promethean, self-sufficient identity, of one's valiantly delusional dreams of conquest in a yet-to-be-colonised wilderness.

In another kōan, not-knowing is presented as blindness:

> Tan Hsia asked a monk, "Where have you come from?" The monk said, "From down the mountain". Hsia said, "Have you eaten yet or not?" The monk said, "I have finished". Hsia said, "Did the person who brought you the food to eat have eyes or not?" The monk was speechless.
>
> Ch'ang Ch'ing asked Pao Fu, "To give someone food to eat is ample requital of the debt of kindness: why wouldn't he have eyes?" Fu said, "Giver and receiver are both blind". Ch'ang Ch'ing said, "If they exhausted their activity, would

> they still turn out blind?" Fu said, "Can you say that I'm blind?" (Cleary & Cleary, 1992: 418)

Many commentaries of this famous kōan focus on degrees of blindness, or 'not-knowing'. *Bonkatsu* is ignorance plain and simple, our ordinary deluded state in the shopping mall of *samsara*. Then there is *jakatsu*, a sort of articulated, well-informed and academic stupidity: we can't experience life simply because of the amount of learned garbage we have accumulated over the years. Next, we have *mikatsu*, the blindness of one who is devoted to practice but is still deluded – too attached, perhaps, to a literal understanding of the teachings. Then there is *shôkatsu* – we begin to grasp that there is nothing to grasp, nothing to see. At last, there is *shinkatsu*, 'true blindness', the point when all talk of liberation and delusion is utterly meaningless.

Seung Sahn said:

> I don't teach Korean or Mahayana or Zen. I don't even teach Buddhism. I only teach *don't know*. Fifty years here and there teaching only *don't know*. So only *don't know*, okay? (Seung, 2009)

Not-knowing begins with disenchantment – a necessary rite of passage, recognising the futility of knowledge, seeing through this fetish of power and acquisition. Disenchantment implies being no longer under the spell, no more subject to the compulsion to own an esoteric/exoteric glossary and a vocabulary of seemingly solid reference points. It means realising how pointless the acquisition of a specialised jargon truly is.

This undermining of knowledge often comes, in Buddhist as in psychotherapeutic circles, with the privileging of a supposedly 'higher' form of expertise. Among Buddhists, this takes the form of 'party tricks', i.e. the fixation with *janas*, with intense and pleasurable states of mental absorption and altered states of consciousness. Among counsellors and psychotherapists, it transposes expertise into 'subtler' domains: the interpersonal, the interpretative and the quasi-mystical notions of 'presence', 'relational depth' and so forth.

Pilgrimage as Encounter

The notion of pilgrimage (*hansan*), central to Dōgen's writings and discourses, refers to both literal journeys (going to a distant monastery in order to meet a teacher and learn from him) and symbolic ones (studying and practising the Dharma). What is common to both is 'encounter'. The Dharma is, for Dōgen, encounter. If it does not reach the heart of ordinary people, our link with the teachings becomes a yoke or, at times, an embellishment. I have to encounter the Dharma, decide for myself to face what Zen calls 'the grave matter of life and death'. I have to go on a pilgrimage and face something entirely other: a teacher, a text, fellow travellers who also undertook this exilarating journey.

This is not the acquisition of esoteric knowledge, the refinement of a particular way of being, the ability to engage in dialectical Dharma combat in the meditation hall (or at dinner parties) nor the attunement to 'presence'. Instead, the accomplished Zen practitioner and/or psychotherapist is on his way to becoming a complete idiot. For it takes an idiot to commit to Dharma practice – a practice which has no purpose and offers no gain. And it takes an even bigger idiot to teach it.

Likewise, it takes an idiot to ask perfectly obvious questions in therapy, the ones, for instance, which Spinelli refers to as "descriptive challenges" (2007: 122-27), requiring a degree of "investigative stillness" in order to challenge "the client's worldview so that its implicit dispositional stances are made more explicit" (ibid: 123).

There cannot be real dialogue without questioning, revisiting and examining anew a worldview, a particular condition or dilemma, the causes and import of a form of anguish.

All our professional training is the springboard for this – creating a relationship of mutual learning where we are both affected, where we can experience the world anew. It sounds easy enough except that it isn't. It is scary, for it means letting go of our knowledge and expertise. Watch this space...

References

Bazzano, M. (2012) *Spectre of the Stranger: towards a Phenomenology of Hospitality*, Academic Press

____ (2013) 'Magnificent Monsters' – Talk given at the 25th Society of Existential Analysis Conference, 23 November, NCVO London, King's Cross

Buchanan, I. (2000) *Deleuzism: A Meta-commentary* (Post-contemporary Interventions) Duke University Press

Cleary, T. (1990) *Book of Serenity*, Lindisfarne Press

Cleary, T. & Cleary, J.C. (1992) *The Blue Cliff Record*, Shambala

Nietzsche, F. (1968) *The Will to Power*, Random House

Nussbaum, M. (2001) *Upheavals of Thought: the Intelligence of Emotions*, Cambridge University Press

Seung, S. (2009) 'Ox Herding: Practice and Daily life', www.bit.ly/notknowing01

Spinelli, E. (2006) *Tales of Unknowing: Therapeutic Encounters from an Existential Perspective*, PCCS Books

____ (2007) *Practising Existential Psychotherapy: the Relational World*, Sage

Surin, K. (2011) 'Existing Not as a Subject But as a Work of Art: The Task of Ethics or Aesthetics?' in Jun, N. & Smith, D.W. (eds). *Deleuze and Ethics*, Edinburgh University Press, pp.142-53

Beginner's Mind

Alex Buchan

> *The method that the Buddha discovered is meditation. He discovered that struggling to find answers doesn't work. It is only when there are gaps in this struggle that insights came to him. He began to realise that there was a sane, awake quality within him which manifested itself only in the absence of struggle. So the practice of meditation involves letting be.*
>
> Chogyam Trungpa Rinpoche quoted in Ray (2004, 7)

Having undertaken my training as a counsellor following an approach that is informed by Buddhism, I want to explore the Buddhist understanding of knowing and not-knowing as a prelude to seeing what relevance, if any, this has for therapy. Such an exploration also has a specific relevance for me because I first stumbled upon Buddhism after I was confronted by a number of setbacks in my life in my late twenties. Looking for answers in various Western models of psychotherapy, I chanced upon the book *Zen Mind, Beginner's Mind* by Shunryu Suzuki. This book was a revelation for me because instead of presenting a methodology, it demonstrated a different way of relating directly to experience. This different way of relating to experience is the hallmark of the Buddhist approach.

The phrase from *Zen Mind, Beginner's Mind* that is most often quoted is: "In the beginner's mind there are many possibilities; in the expert's mind there are few". The wording is important because it points to an inherent problem in the self-perception of the expert. From a Zen Buddhist point of view, the problem with the acquisition of knowledge is that we invariably identify with our knowledge, and this acts in very subtle ways to block us from experiencing things in an open, un-predetermined way. This was realised by the Buddha himself long before Buddhism arrived in Japan. In my own fumbling way, it also proved true for me. In this article I want to discuss this important idea of Buddhist thinking: attachment to views. In order to do this, I will need to give some background as to how the Buddha came up with this elusive idea and how he succeeded in communicating it to others. Then I will discuss my own experiences of trying to come to terms with this notion. In doing so, I hope to convey how the Buddha's great insight continues to be valid thousands of years after it was first conceived.

Origins of Right View

The early Buddhist *Kalakarama Sutta* is a good way into understanding the Buddha's analysis of 'knowing'. In this sutra the Buddha describes his own relationship to knowing. The language, at least as translated into English, appears very abstruse, mostly because the sutra is trying to communicate something extremely difficult to understand. First, the Buddha goes through every permutation of knowing and not-knowing, to make it clear that he does, in fact, know all that there is to know. Yet he does not take a stand on it. He then explains what he does not do in relation to the thing known or apprehended by the senses (which include the mind as a sense organ). The same essential explanation applies for each sense faculty. For cognising, referring to himself as a *Tathagata* – one who has realised the truth – he makes the following statement:

> ...[a *Tahthagata*] does not conceive of a cognisable thing as apart from cognition; he does not conceive of the uncognised; he does not conceive of a 'thing worth cognising'; he does not conceive about one who cognises.

The Buddha, in other words, is pointing to the psychological dynamic of knowing whereby we grasp at conceptual understanding and become enmeshed in the idea that if only we could understand something our problems would be solved. This he links to our investment in the idea of a thing worth 'cognising' and to our attachment to the idea of being one who knows. In the concluding verse, presented below, he describes all of these ways of attaching to views as barbs on which people become caught.

> Whatever is seen, heard, sensed or clung to,
> is esteemed as truth by other folk,
> Midst those who are entrenched in their own views,
> being 'Such' I hold none as true or false.
>
> This barb I beheld, well in advance,
> whereon mankind are hooked, impaled.

> "I know, I see, 'tis verily so" –
> no such clinging for the tathagatas.
> *Anguttara Nikaya II. 24ff.* (trans. Bhikkhu Nananda, 1997)

This raises an important question both for scholars of early Buddhism and for contemporary Buddhist practitioners. If attachment to views is a barb on which we are in danger of finding ourselves ensnared, how can we view a path that will lead to liberation?

Paul Fuller in his book on the Buddhist understanding of views has written that: "This notion of 'view' or 'opinion' (*ditthi*) as an obstacle to 'seeing things as they are' (*yathābhūtadassana*) is a central concept in Buddhist thought." However, defining the early Buddhist understanding of views is complicated by the fact that two apparently different approaches seem to be taken. The "texts talk about 'wrong' and 'right' view and the aim of the path as the cultivation of 'right-view' and the abandonment of 'wrong view'." But there are also texts which seem to suggest that the aim of the Buddhist path is to overcome "all views, even right views, because any view, if held with attachment, can be a wrong view." Drawing on an article by Rupert Gethin, Fuller believes these differences are more apparent than real, and sees both positions as pointing to something more difficult to articulate (Fuller, 2005, 1). To illuminate this matter further, I want to turn to Gethin. Having reviewed the register of terms used to describe 'views' in early Buddhist Theravada texts, he concludes:

> While there is certainly some notion of the wrong, mistaken and false content of 'view' in this treatment, two related notions seem to dominate: first, that view is something that we hold on to, cling to and that thus becomes rigid and fixed; second, that view is something we get stuck in, tangled in and lost in. (2004, 22)

This tendency for all views to lead to attachment is something we will look at when we look at the problems experienced by many of us who are drawn to Buddhist practice. But even though he mainly addresses scholars, Gethin offers a useful and practical insight in his discussion that any practitioner can use:

> Since Buddhist texts furnish *micchā ditthi* (wrong view) with formal content, it is all too tempting... to assume that *sammā ditthi* (right view) has a formal content that is precisely the

> inverse of *micchā ditthi* and that right view thus… consists in assent to the claim that things are impermanent, suffering and not-self, to the claim that… the cause of suffering is craving, the cessation of suffering is the cessation of craving and that the way leading to the cessation of suffering is the eightfold path. (ibid: 24)

Gethin believes the problem is due to the reluctance of scholars to refer to the Abhidamma texts which draw on and synthesise the material in the sutras; a reluctance, which, he says, runs counter to the high esteem in which these texts are held by the Buddhist tradition itself. The Abhidamma, or Further Doctrine, which was developed by Buddhist scholars in the early centuries after the Buddha's death, distilled his teachings in a highly systematised form. On the basis of Abhidamma passages, Gethin argues, "*sammā-ditthi* (right view) is never to be conceived of as a correct opinion or belief". Instead ordinary right view, understood as *panna* (wisdom), is a mental concomitant of ordinary virtuous consciousness, as "when we give a gift or turn away from harming a living creature or taking what is not given". Right view is therefore seen as that which informs our ethical behaviour. But from the perspective of the Abhidamma, this can never be due merely to adherence to a set of beliefs. Gethin's understanding is that it should instead be understood as the result of seeing into the nature of things directly.

> From the perspective of Abhidhamma, what we generally refer to as belief or opinion must, I think, be analysed as the occurrence of a state of mind in which there is an attachment or clinging to some proposition or theory. If that attachment is directed towards a proposition generally approved by the Buddhist tradition – a proposition such as 'actions have results' – then there is a sense in which the belief or opinion might be regarded, from the Buddhist viewpoint, as 'correct belief'; but such a state of mind remains quite different from actually seeing that actions have results. (ibid: 25)

Returning to the *Kalakarama Sutta* we can see that what the sutra is pointing to is anything that we add to such direct experiencing. The sutra uses the phrase "as apart from cognition", and in the cases of the other senses, as apart from seeing, hearing, smelling, tasting and touching. What the sutra is highlighting is the connection between conceiving of a self and the resulting distortion of perception and conception. Conceiving of a self in this context means identifying with our feelings, associations and thought processes and engaging with experience from a personal standpoint based on that identification. What lies behind this need to coalesce around our thoughts and feelings is our deep-rooted fear of being open and vulnerable and it is this which Buddhism describes as stopping us from seeing things in an impartial way. This does not mean ignoring our feelings, associations or various trains of thought, but rather having some spaciousness or detachment in our relation to them, so that they can be related to without carrying us away. This in essence is what Buddhist practice seeks to do. For Buddhism, this experiencing directly, without attachment, means seeing things correctly in an undistorted way. In Buddhism, even *sammā ditthi* or Right View, if grasped at, leads to the fabrication of an idealised self. It is right only to the extent to which it points to and facilitates this direct experience of the truth. So it is in this way that the two apparently opposing positions on views are reconciled.

This needs to be understood in the historical context in which the Buddha lived. Buddhism, at its most basic, represented a new vision of human dignity. It opposed the orthodox views of Brahmins that dominated India at the time, as well as the doctrines of other rival religious philosophies. The Buddha rejected the scriptural authority of the Vedas and all points of view stemming from it, which he expressed in a comprehensive, three pronged critique. In religious practice, he rejected all deisms and all forms of sacrifice as means of finding salvation; intellectually, he rejected the idea of a Self (*Atman*), which was the at the heart of Brahmin metaphysics; and in a deeply sexist society which was structured on caste, original Buddhism asserted women's spiritual equality with men and rejected the caste system as an indicator of spiritual worth, accepting even untouchables into the monastic order with the same status as former kings. Its rejection of caste is illustrated by a noteworthy episode recounted in the Pali Canon. Once, the Buddha met an untouchable, whose caste duty was to dispose of excrement. He wanted to join the sangha. The Buddha brought him to the edge of a river and after washing him himself, then accepted this untouchable into the monastic community, despite the loud protests of others. (Hahn, 1995: 37) But Buddhism has primarily been understood not as a critique of all belief systems, but as a separate, rival belief system in its own right. While there are good reasons for regarding Buddhism in this way, doing so overlooks the deconstructive efforts of the Buddha to find the truth of experience by ridding it of ideological filters. This divorce of

Buddhism from its context is explained well by K. R. Norman; a philologist, who specialises in the middle Indic languages of the Early Buddhist texts:

> ...it is hard to see why almost all writers about Buddhism accept the statement often made that the Buddha makes no mention of the Upanisadic concept of a Universal Self, an *atman* or *brahman*. When the Buddha stated that everything was *anatta* 'not self', we should expect that the view of *atta* 'self', which he was denying, was that held by other teachers at that time. We can, in fact, deduce, from what the Buddha rejected, the doctrine which the other teachers upheld. (Norman, 1997: 26)

Norman points out that *anatta* is almost universally mistranslated by writers on Buddhism, and references the following examples: "unreal", "non-substantial", "without self", "ego-less" and "having no soul". All of these presuppose a Buddhist philosophical position. However, "the grammar and syntax show that *anatta* is not a possessive adjective, which it would need to be to support such a meaning". *Anatta* is a descriptive compound, and, as those things which the Buddha refers to as *anatta* are sometimes referred to as *parato*, i.e. "as other", then the only translation which can ever be correct is 'not self'. This is important because it shows that the Buddha was not simply proposing a counter view to the prevalent view of the time. Instead, the Buddha's advice to regard everything as impermanent, unsatisfactory and not self was intended to help us stay open to our experience without getting snared in identification.

Norman uses another example from the early Buddhist texts to demonstrate that the Buddha's intent was to clarify his opposition to the Upanisadic idea that the self as *atman* and the cosmos as *brahman* reflect a non-dual reality. "The Buddha asked his followers whether, when they saw wood being burned, they felt any pain. The answer was 'No', and the explanation given was that they did not feel any pain because the wood was not part of the self." (ibid: 27) The Buddhist understanding of truth is therefore not about the truth of propositions; it is primarily about the truth of our individual experiences. More to the point, it is about finding lasting freedom from within individual experience.

Viewing the Path

Now I can use my own experience to show the extent to which this attachment to knowing outlined by the Buddha pervades our lives and is present in the pursuit of Buddhist practice itself. When I came upon *Zen Mind, Beginner's Mind*, I had accumulated a series of disappointments and setbacks and was searching for answers. Though it wasn't clear to me at the time, the book put me back in touch with a sense of wonder that I had experienced as a child whenever I felt misunderstood and used to escape into a nearby wood where I felt I could be fully myself. This renewed contact with wonder helped me to get back into the flow of life. But, when, some years later as a teenager I ran into fresh difficulties, I felt I needed to master my life more fully and went through a phase of intense searching for an understanding which I thought would finally solve my problems. I started to attend a meditation group and read every book on Zen I could find.

This process culminated in an experience of mine as a young adult which happened one morning when I locked myself out of my flat without car keys or money. For me, this seemed to stand as an indictment of all my fraudulent attempts to emulate the enlightenment ideals that I had been reading about. In a state of self-recrimination, I set out to walk to work across the city on a route that took me through a large city park. Walking under majestic trees my mood suddenly began to change and I felt a sense of contrition for my self-preoccupation. So I vowed to turn my attention outward to those I encountered by seeing the Buddha nature in everyone I saw. No sooner had I entertained this thought than all illusion seemed to fall away and I saw everything as it actually is. This was the illumination, the *kensho* that Zen Buddhists see as the gateway to enlightenment and that I had all but despaired of ever finding. At that moment, I realised that all my efforts to pursue understanding had stopped me from being open to the truth. But now, no longer trying to cognise, I was truly able to see.

Many years later, when I had travelled to Taiwan to practice Chan – Zen in its Chinese form – I had a similar insight. Wandering so far in pursuit of a truth, I came to realise that illumination could actually be found anywhere in almost any situation. But this realisation was disrupted by other matters which were outside of my control and took me back to Britain. Nevertheless, my realisation in Taiwan was still working on me when I made an important vow to always stay in meditation centres. In retrospect, I think this set in motion a chain of events that first led me to try to stay at Plum Village, Thich Nhat Hanh's monastery in France. Unfortunately, once there I found that the winter period was closed to all non-monastics due to building work and my spiritual quest seemed to be thwarted. But just as I made this deflating discovery I happened to meet a German fellow who had also wanted to stay at Plum Village. He suggested going to Karma Ling, a Tibetan monastery in the Alps where we might be able spend the winter in retreat. Having nothing better to do, I thought: "Why not?" He immediately made the arrangements for us to undertake extended solitary retreats there. When we arrived, there was a torrential rainstorm, but my heart was full of anticipation and joy. Once again I had a feeling of being in the flow of my life's purpose and I eagerly threw myself into study and practice. But after a while a problem arose: I seemed to be getting nowhere. As had been the case all those years before, I once again found myself chasing after understanding. Still, although I was discouraged, I was not about to quit.

One day, as I sat in meditation trying to maintain what I had convinced myself was the Tibetan advanced meditation technique called *mahamudra*, I became aware that my ordinary awareness had somehow detached from this process. And when I opened up to it, my ordinary awareness had turned into a natural effortless mindfulness. This uncontrived state arose spontaneously without any struggle at all. I remained in this state of natural mindfulness, which was present whether I was meditating or not, for another two weeks until thoughts about what I would do after the retreat led to its weakening and eventual disappearance. But the memory of the experience has remained with me ever since.

These experiences gave me a different understanding of the traditional accounts of the Buddha's life story. In the original Pali discourses the Buddha speaks of the turning point which led to his enlightenment thus:

> I thought: 'I recall once, when my father the Sakyan was working, and I was sitting in the cool shade of a rose-apple tree, then – quite withdrawn from sensuality, withdrawn from unskillful mental qualities – I entered and remained in the first jhana: rapture and pleasure born from withdrawal, accompanied by directed thought and evaluation. Could that be the path to Awakening?' Then, following on that memory, came the realization: 'That is the path to Awakening'. I thought: 'So why am I afraid of that pleasure that has nothing to do with sensuality, nothing to do with unskillful mental qualities?' *Majjhima Nikaya 36*, (trans. Thanissaro Bhikkhu)

In this sequence of thoughts the Buddha becomes aware of his own chasing after something external. Aware that he had, in fact, been denying his own direct experience in favour of what he had regarded as the received wisdom which was that attachment to the body had to be broken through the practice of austerities. The Buddha's quest had been initiated by deep feeling of unease about a life built on denial of the reality of impermanence and death. He intuited that a more noble life was possible. This combination of faith and questioning and great determination is evident in the accounts of his experiences before his enlightenment.

The Buddhist scriptures describe how the Buddha practised meditation under two teachers, Alara Kalama and Udaka Ramaputta. Scholars used to accept the French Buddhologist André Bareau's opinion that the story about the Buddha's two teachers was a fabrication. But recent scholarship casts doubt on his claim as the traditional account has been corroborated by other evidence (Wynne, 2007). While staying with both teachers, the Buddha-to-be, having mastered the advanced meditation practices and directly experienced them, is depicted as reflecting:

> But the thought occurred to me, 'This [meditative practice] leads not to disenchantment, to dispassion, to cessation, to stilling, to direct knowledge, to Awakening.' (ibid)

In other words, the Buddha was guided by his deep need to find the answer to the question of suffering, which led him to experiment with a variety of meditative techniques and disciplines, but he found none of them satisfactory. When he turned to practising austerities, his approach was to pursue them to the extreme until his question would finally be answered. But then, when he became aware of just how close to death he was, yet no nearer to finding the answer he sought, there was a loosening of his zeal and a space opened up within him in which the memory of his childhood experience was allowed to arise. And with it came the realisation that the truth had been available to him all along if only he had had faith in his own direct experience.

This has important implications not only for me as a practising Buddhist, but also as a counsellor who tries to draw on Buddhist wisdom in my professional work. For my spiritual practice, it's largely a matter of putting my ideas to the side and allowing myself to abide in the natural spaciousness of the Buddha mind which pervades all things. I can only try to set favourable conditions to allow the Buddha mind to emerge. I can't force it by an act of will or by adhering slavishly even to my best ideas of how Buddhism should be practised. I have to let the Buddha-mind be, instead of trying to become my ideal of it.

And, in counselling, what I try to do is help my clients discover that direct experience of their basic nature isn't something to be afraid of. Ultimately, it is what liberates and heals, though it does require sensitivity and persistence to negotiate the obstacles that block their view of it. This can be compared to what the Buddha himself did after his enlightenment. At first, he thought his realisation was too difficult and subtle to be communicated to people. But then, after hearing a request from the god Brahma to teach those "with a little dust in their eyes", he embarked on his mission as a spiritual teacher. Counselling isn't the same as a spiritual practice and I am certainly not a teacher like the Buddha. But most of my life has been spent with dust in my eyes, yet in some rare and precious moments I have been able to see. In truth, anybody can see once they lose their attachment to views.

References

Bhikkhu K. Nanananda (1997) *The Magic of the Mind*, Pariyatti Press

Fuller, P. (2005) *The Notion of ditthi in Theravada Buddhism: The Point of View*, Routledge Curzon

Gethin, R. (2004) 'Wrong view (miccha-ditthi) and right view (samma-ditthi) in the Theravada Abhidhamma', *Contemporary Buddhism* Vol. 5, No 1

Nhat Hanh, T. (1995) *Zen Keys: a guide to zen practice*, Thorsons

Norman, K. R. (1997) 'A Philological Approach to Buddhism', *The Buddhist Forum* Vol. 5, School of Oriental and African Studies

Ray, R. A. (2004) *In the Presence of Masters*, Shambala

Suzuki, S. (1970) *Zen Mind, Beginner's Mind*, Weatherhill

Thanissaro Bhikkhu (trans.) (2008) 'Maha-Saccaka Sutta: The Longer Discourse to Saccaka' MN 36 PTS: M I 237, www.bit.ly/notknowing05

Wynne, A (2007) *The Origins of Buddhist Meditation*, Routledge

Ghosts

Mia Livingston

As a Zen trainee I learned that all fears, great and small, can be traced to a single root cause: the fear of death. Not necessarily physical death, but the death of life as we know it. A disruption to everyday comforts and routines, for example, can sometimes easily poke holes in the sense of self that we have spent years building up.

Such a disruption can be as subtle as a sense of unease when I find myself alone in an empty apartment. In turning towards that unease and examining it closely, rather than turning away, I found resolution. This is my story about how I stopped being afraid of the dark.

When night falls, I sometimes stop myself from automatically reaching for the light switch. Instead I watch inky darkness slowly submerge each room of my apartment, as if I am sinking and everything is sinking with me. As I stand at my windows, the last of the daylight wanes into a pale distant line. Above the skylight there is a rising moon.

In the absence of light, my ears prick up. The hum of cars outside and the creaks of the old building, moving imperceptibly and stiffly like joints of an aging body, stand out in relief. An unfamiliar bird calls from the roof.

There is a kind of freedom in not seeing. Just a few hours ago this was my home: the place where I could take everything for granted. At home I pay the bills, take phone calls, do the dishes and the laundry. But now – for all my eyes know – I could be anywhere.

In the corner of the room, a large curved outline crouches. It has a gentle light on the upper and right side, but remains dark underneath and all around. My physical instinct is to stay still and watch it keenly, waiting to see if it moves.

I notice, to my surprise, that I am barely breathing. My chest and stomach muscles are tense, as if they are ready to throw my body sideways. Consciously I take the deepest in- and out-breath that I can. I imagine my body inhaling the dark. *Nothing to be afraid of,* I think. Based on where the outline is resting like a nocturnal animal, and the fact that it has not yet moved, it is likely to only be a piece of furniture, I think.

I don't believe in ghosts.

Let me rephrase that. I believe that if a boundary exists between the safe and the visible on the one hand, and the unsafe and invisible on the other, because of that personal judgement call, whether 'ghosts' exist or not depends on our subjective viewpoint. They cannot be said to absolutely exist.

In every moment, every form of life arises and decays; it is born, and dies. I feel the internal movements of my body as I write, arising and falling. I see nature's turnover in the leaves in the wind. In modern Western culture, we are accustomed to noticing only one side of that cycle: that which is alive in the same sense that we currently are. But what about the other side of the cycle, that which we say is dead? Does death necessarily mean non-existence? And if it does, do we have to fear it?

A handful of times I have seen inexplicable shadows and fogs indoors, where the stable light conditions and closed curtains meant that there was no other movement that could account for what I saw. The visions were accompanied by a feeling of cold.

The first time I saw an apparition clearly was two weeks before my niece died at birth, strangled by her own umbilical cord. In the half-light of the evening in my room in London, I woke with a start without knowing why. Then I saw a dark figure standing over my bed. It gave the impression of a masculine solidity and strength, and was standing over my stomach, holding what looked like a raised axe, as dark as the figure itself.

My reaction was as you might expect: I gasped for air. I screamed and no sound came out. My body was rigid and cold with fear. I was aware that it was evening and that the light could be playing tricks on my eyes, so with my mouth open I stared and stared at what I saw, looking for light and shadow-play, desperately willing it to be otherwise. For some reason my body would not move so I knew that if the figure decided to act, there would be nothing I could do. Finally I managed to gasp, "what do you want?" The figure dissolved before my eyes until there was nothing there.

Five years later, a second apparition appeared. I was staying in a hut by the beach, and woke – again in the half-light – to a dark figure standing by my bedside. Intuitively I knew that it was not of human form, and that it was observing me. But this time was different. It was at the foot of my bed, and its arms were docile at its sides. As the previous one had, this one had a solid 'masculine' energy; but it was more delicate, and not aggressive.

Quietly in my mind I asked if it was threatening, and the answer I received was that it was not.

The following morning I received news that my cherished uncle, who was in his 70s, had died peacefully in the night.

While the two events were not definitive, my curiosity was awakened. Over the next four years I sought out teachers who taught me how to see that which is not normally seen in our culture. I experienced events in sober and broad daylight which showed me beyond my own doubt, at least, that time does not always run in a straight and neat line from 'past' to 'future'; and that we can know things which our ordinary five senses have not yet understood.

But along the way, I also learned that preoccupation with the unknown is a sidetrack. At worst, seekers sought to manipulate others with their new-found powers and understanding; at best, it was an entertaining diversion. For me curiosity was healthy, but it wasn't enough. It needed conscious direction. I sought the peace which I could see in the movements of the Zen masters I had met.

A heart can only be at peace when it trusts that that which it needs to know, is not being withheld. The nature of life is not a secret. Events and memories find their way to the surface of our awareness when they, and we, are ready. We are not subjective beings in an objective world. We arise together with the world, and ultimately there is no separation. I believe that when I fear events and beings in the perceived world, I am fearing myself.

I first learned to let go out of necessity. As a young woman, partly out of curiosity and partly frustration with a pervasive sense of 'stuckness', I signed up to hike and work across the jungles of Borneo. It was a basic hand-to-mouth existence where the wrong decision or a single instance of bad luck could mean the difference between life and death. Over six weeks the group leader, a former Royal Marine commando officer, taught us how to live on the razor's edge – and eventually even to play there. So long as we were together, we learned, there was nothing to fear. It is the man who sets out on his own, who is in real danger. All successful soldiers, we were told, know this.

Nights in the jungle were thick with the unknown. The humidity and insect life were so pervasive that my skin was always trickling either with sweat or with six-legged visitors. Eventually I stopped caring which. After a hard day's hike and work we would huddle in the safety of the group around a bonfire.

One night I needed to visit the latrine, which was fifty metres away at the edge of the camp. Fifty metres is nothing at home in broad daylight. But when you're alone in the jungle and afraid of the dark, it is potentially life-changing. A colleague had once lost his bearings on a similar occasion. The thick foliage quickly closed off visibility and acoustics, until he could no longer find his way back. He spent three frantic days on his own facing the end of his life, before the group finally tracked him down.

I walked as far as the edge of the makeshift shelters before shining my weak pocket torch towards a single set of planks which were laid across the swamp. The small hum of the group's talk seemed impossibly far away, dwarfed by the sharp insects' calls from somewhere much closer to my body. A smell of decay rose with the heat from the resting earth.

The last time I had felt that vulnerable I had been a child, alone in my room and afraid of the dark. I was still afraid. Who knew what dwells in the spaces into which we cannot see? It could be anything. Rational thought cannot touch the infinite creativity that is born from fear. All the horror film scenes I had ever seen conspired to hover just over my head, waiting to intrude in my weakest moment. Only a few decades earlier this land had been used for head hunting.

The plank I was balancing on sank slightly into the swamp. One false step and I could fall into the peat, breaking a leg or worse. The group would assume I had gone to bed and would not discover me until the morning. I had already sustained an infected shin wound which cut to the bone from falling through a rotten railway plank two days earlier.

It was impossible to imagine that the morning would ever come. It was as foreign to my situation as a different planet, when all was engulfed in darkness. Instead, a breeze crossed my face. Boughs creaked and strange animals called.

Suddenly I felt weary. I was tired of being afraid. I recalled my mother's reasoning voice whenever I had refused as a child to move at night: "Everything is exactly the same in the dark, as it was a few hours ago. It's just that you can't see it - but nothing's changed."

I realised that the fear was not out of control – it was of my own making. I made a decision which would serve me for the rest of my life. Whether ghosts and malevolence existed or not, thinking of them would not help me. By force of will I un-thought them, and concentrated only on what I knew. I had nothing to lose.

Ok, what do I really know? I know that I am in my body right now. I feel my feet on the wooden path, and I hear my breath. The skin on my arms is sticky. Mosquitoes are nibbling like pin pricks on my ankles and on the backs of my hands. An opaque restless oval of fear stretches inside, from my lower stomach to my chest. It shifts and turns, looking every which way, as if my organs were a writhing nest of snakes with gleaming eyes. But that's ok. It's only a feeling. Feelings can't kill me.

When the imaginary snakes realised they would not be entertained, they soon went back to sleep. The space in front of me somehow opened up. I had cleared a space in my mind which changed what I saw. The only movement now was a gentle, almost fresh, breeze. I had been afraid of my own thoughts, and learned that they were my own creation. In the most understated way, I felt free. My story was empty.

The ancient people whom the Buddha originally taught did not discern as rigidly between inner imagination and an external world, and even today there are many cultures that embrace the possibility of ghosts. But while I could banish ghosts with a sleight of mind, the possibility of crashing into solid objects – and the instinct to survive by avoiding them – were all real.

A writer who became blind in an accident in childhood, Jacques Lusseyran, discovered that if he let go of the shadow side of his own willpower, the physical universe was revealed to him without the need for eyesight. In his book *And There Was Light* he writes,

> Being blind I thought I should have to go out and meet things, but I found that they came to meet me instead. The substance of the universe drew together… a radiance emanating from a place I knew nothing about.
>
> It is a tuning in and allowing the current they hold to connect with one's own, like electricity. This means an end of living in front of things, and a beginning of living with them.

When my mind relaxed because I had stopped worrying about falling and all the consequences of falling, my body had the freedom to discover its own intelligence. My foot did not need the eyes in my head, in order to know that there was a tree root ahead that it needed to step over. Bodies know more things than I had given them credit for.

The dark and I became friends, after that.

Back in my apartment in the city, every now and then I call back the ghost of my memory to teach me again. I leave the lights off when darkness falls, and welcome it. As I see it now, I am not a person alone in a room. Rather the space of the room embraces me, allowing my spirit to nestle into it as if it were a comfortable bed. The fact that ultimately there are no boundaries – that over time, all forms inexorably rise and fall with and into each other – becomes more noticeable when I can no longer see where my body ends, and other forms begin. Darkness holds its own kind of poetry. Even if there are ghosts, there is no need to fear them.

As darkness falls, it invites us to completely be ourselves. The thousand judgements which I and others make every day based on appearances, can no longer exist. Without a demarcation between imagination and reality, the possibility of who we are opens up. As I walk down a darkened street it does not care whether I am a man or woman, young or old, crippled or an athlete. Those labels were imposed both from the inside and out, but they don't always have to be.

Whatever You Think, It's More Than That

Ian Finlay

When the Buddha was asked whether there was a God or not, he famously observed a "noble silence". Later, when asked why he had not answered, he explained that any answer given would be confusing, that he would have been 'taking sides' in the debate that was going on at the time. Perhaps though, that silence was answer in itself, for we live in a world that craves certainty, understanding, explanation and meaning for our lives. This is perhaps why practically every people, from the most 'primitive' Amazonian Indian or New Guinea tribe, has had a religion, a system that explains existence (Smart, 1976).

And most religions explain everything very well. For there are everywhere creation myths, each of which tells what happened before we were born and what will happen when we die. The fact that these myths don't all quite agree with each other may be beside the point. I would argue that the deepest truth, and the real religion – in the original sense of re-connection (from the Latin, *religio*) – is not-knowing; that somehow if we hold ourselves in this moment, where we have no answers to anything, then we are close to the source of life itself, whence all creation springs.

Of course, it is not only religions that attempt to give meaning to our lives. Science is a modern attempt to explain our universe and is no doubt successful in explaining many physical phenomena. But as a retired professor of physics said to me the other day, "We don't really know anything. Even if the big bang theory is right, what came before the big bang?" His comment reminded me of the old conundrum: "If God made the universe, then who made God?" Such questions always bring me up short, for I realise that there is no answer to them. There is always a step beyond the problems that science addresses and the thinking mind alone cannot answer the most fundamental questions: where did we come from? Where do we go when we die? Why do we have this inner consciousness, a world of feelings and emotions that is so deeply enmeshed in an outer world that is perhaps even more unfathomable? As my favourite musicians, The Incredible String Band, sang, "Whatever you think, it's more than that!"

Richard Dawkins mentions the awe that he felt as a boy when he contemplated nature, "tearful with the unheard music of the Milky Way". He says these feelings are common amongst scientists and rationalists and describes them, perhaps somewhat disparagingly, as "quasi-mystical experiences". It was this sense of wonder that led him to science and I certainly relate to that, for I too find nature amazing: the tiny eels in the streams that have swum all the way from the Sargasso Sea; the migrations of butterflies; the orchids that mimic female bees to get pollinated. Or just being in the wild wood where I spend much of my time, aware of the gentle swaying of hundred-foot-tall trees in the wind. I am filled with a sense of wonder, a sense of being that goes beyond narrow definitions of self. I would not be ashamed to call this feeling of deep relationship to nature a form of mystical experience. Very often, it seems, these experiences can only come when the thinking mind is 'dropped' (as Buddhists might say) and we can be and act in spontaneous accord with nature. In building a stone wall, for example, one can search and dig for exactly the right stone and become frustrated when none seems to meet one's preconceived specifications. But, to borrow an image that the Buddha himself used (Dhammapada, vv. 153-4), when the builder of self, who is also the slave of his own designs, disappears, so often the right stone appears and the wall will seem to build itself.

Zen kōans point to this experience. I once worked on the kōan 'how is life fulfilled?'. I struggled for days, thinking it was about my life: how is *my* life fulfilled. Then the penny dropped. It was not about my life. It was about life, and life is fulfilled all the time. There is nothing I can do about it. This was made clear to me when I was once sitting outside my hut in a tropical rainforest waiting for my interview with my Zen teacher, the Japanese master Hogen Roshi. I sat thinking, working out everything I was going to say to him, then hearing his bell and walking barefoot across the forest floor, my head full of the answers I was going to give him. Upon reaching his hut I bowed low then gasped in horror as I noticed a huge leech gorging on my toe. The teacher knocked it off with a piece of wood and it went looping off across the clearing. I burst out laughing, all my thoughts and answers completely blown away. Such a lesson was so much more real than any ideas I might have had about Zen and enlightenment. "Whatever you think, it's more than that." Or, from another point of view, perhaps so much less.

In fact working with Hogen-san was a continual challenge for me to be in the here and now, accepting the totally unexpected. The examples I could give are many. We always used to go for a run in the early morning and once came across a children's playground, whereupon we all had to follow Hogen as he climbed to the top of the slides and slid down and played on the swings! Or on another occasion we were running backwards down a Devon lane at 5.30 in the morning. The rest of us all heard the sound of a motor approaching, but Hogen, who suffered from the cold and was wearing earmuffs, did not. So to our horror a somewhat shocked local milkman suddenly found a Japanese Zen master sprawled across the bonnet of his truck. Fortunately, no harm was done and a laughing Hogen picked himself up and carried on. My memories of Hogen are of tremendous presence coupled with absolute unconditional acceptance and compassion. But he also had a childlike quality that reminds me of Jesus's saying about becoming as little children before we can enter the kingdom of heaven.

But one does not have to go to a tropical rainforest to find a leech for a good teaching or have unexpected and bizarre experiences in Devon lanes. The teachings are all around. We can hear them in the cry of the buzzard, the plaintive note of the curlew or the sweet song of the thrush. Like the wakeup bird in Aldous Huxley's *Island* they can all bring us back to our true nature and the mystery of being. These sounds of nature seem particularly significant to me, for through them I am often brought back into the wonder of this present moment as I walk the hills and woods of Wales. The power of nature as opposed to the intellectual efforts of men has been acknowledged by mystics through the ages, especially in the East.

> 'You've travelled up a thousand steps in search of the dharma,
> So many days in the archives, copying, copying
> The gravity of the Tang, the profundity of the Sung make heavy baggage
> Here! I've picked you a bunch of wildflowers,
> Their meaning is the same,
> But they are much easier to carry'.
>
> (Xu Yun)

Or as the contemporary Western singer/songwriter Robin Williamson put it, "All that the wise men can say, the birds sing".

But being and working with nature is not romanticism. Every time I walk through my woods I am confronted by death. A dead woodcock, entrails spilling out, part-eaten by a fox, or small mammals, maybe victims of owls or polecats, always give me a slight shock and remind me that as I get older my own time here is running out. I have lived much of my life as if I was eternal, planning for the future that would never end. But now I am aware that I must face the great mystery of my passing. How will it be? How will I go? It is not that I want to go, far from it. I love this life now perhaps more than I have ever done, but I also feel less concerned at the thought of leaving it. I certainly have no particular faith in the certainty of the resurrection or anything else, but I have a strange confidence. If I can fully accept this moment with all its mystery and unknowing, I will somehow be able to accept future moments with all their mystery and unknowing.

In fact it has come to me that certainty may be a form of death, or suicide, as it precludes any form of growth, of real living: dead certainty, indeed. I even find myself uneasy at all the things I thought I believed in. Recently at a gathering to discuss climate change and ecological destruction I found myself getting increasingly uncomfortable. We all agreed how terrible it was, how we are facing catastrophe and those who thought otherwise were undoubtedly indoctrinated by consumerist advertising and the propaganda of the oil industry. But what about us? I thought. Is it not possible that we have our own indoctrination, our own agendas that might be preventing us from recognising other, more favourable possibilities?

It seems we cannot know anything for certain and everything is subject(ive) to our own consciousness and way of seeing things. We do not even know what the 'I' is that does the knowing. We talk of the 'I' almost as a third person (I am doing it myself), as if there are two 'I's: one that acts in the world and another that can dispassionately observe the first 'I'. Most people quite understandably like to feel they know who and what they are, for there is a great sense of security in that knowing. Yet knowing who we are is not the same as knowing what we are, and not knowing either seems to be our ultimate truth. I freely confess that for much of my life I have been one of those people who sought security in a fixed identity. In fact it was very much my own desperate insecurity that led me to study Zen and the mystics. Long periods of the most severe depression, terrible confusion and feelings of isolation and despair, not knowing who I was – I suffered these all. Those feelings have long left me, but I still suffer from bouts of extreme insomnia, which, though terrible while they last, remind me that I am not in control, that I am not, perhaps, quite as content as I thought I was. A lesson in humility, that for all my attainment and wisdom, the incredibly wise things I am writing about at the moment (!) will have to be given up, for the intellectual understanding, even of the so-called deepest truths, is a trap and no substitute for the actual experience of not-knowing.

Now I increasingly find that this not-knowing is a place of adventure, creativity and honesty. It is a place where we accept the here and now, things as they are without preconceptions; where we can die and be reborn each second. This seems to me to be what many scriptures from different traditions are talking about, that creation is not something out there, separate from us, but something we can continuously participate in. All we have to do is let go, have the courage to forget all that we thought we knew, to climb to the top of that Zen pole and take that one step further, to let ourselves go into that 'cloud of unknowing' (if I may mix metaphors from different traditions). It is there that the real revelation occurs, where we leave certainty behind and enter the great mystery, where "love knocks and knowledge stands without" (St Buenaventura). It is there that we not only come to know nothing, but truly know "no thing", as we "pass beyond everything into unknowing" (St John of the Cross). In that place we might be "holy fools" or the '"little children" that Christ spoke of. There we would no longer be condemned to live a half-life with our security and set beliefs, but dwell in a total not-knowing, regaining the lost Eden before we ate of the fruit of that tree of knowledge, an act which was fatal for our innocence. Perhaps in recovering the innocence of not-knowing we might truly enter a kingdom of heaven where every moment is fresh and pure and is a revelation in itself.

But already I have said far too much. My words and thoughts are as last year's dead leaves that are blown by the wind on the path. It is a sunny day. Shadows play across the garden as the wind stirs the trees. A bumblebee collects nectar from the fading camellia blossoms. The blue tits that nest in my wall are busy feeding their young. And somewhere a robin sings. Have we the eyes and the ears to see and to hear?

References

2007, *The Dhammapada,* Nilgiri Press

Smart, N. (1976) *The Religious Experience of Mankind,* Scribner

Collective Not-Knowing and its Innate Potential

Andy Paice

In order to find our way, we must get lost

African proverb

Retreat into Group Process

There were fifteen of us, men with shaven heads, most in our late twenties or early thirties, wearing maroon robes, sitting attentively in a state of exhausted frustration around a large dining table in a farmhouse in the rural Auvergne, France. We were Buddhist monastics in the middle of a traditional Tibetan 3-year closed retreat. Our group had been going through a rough patch. Issues around a breakdown in trust about respecting retreat rules had emerged. The talking was interminable to the extent that we'd stopped going to our daily meditation sessions. An open wound had appeared in our group and we knew we had to heal it so that our minds could settle and allow us to get on with our practice. But we just didn't know how. So we continued talking, each person saying his piece, doing his best to speak from the heart; and when we were too exhausted we stopped, took a break or had a meal. I remember this period seemed to last for days and, as it progressed, things deepened. Each person in turn opened up, revealing new aspects of himself – to the group and to himself. We had unexpectedly found ourselves in a gut-wrenching process with no idea of where it was heading. We just knew we had to go on talking and purging; and the Western lamas who were guiding our retreat encouraged us to do just that.

With nothing to do other than sit in our collective emotional stew, new insights slowly emerged, a new spirit of transparency materialised and breakthroughs in communication emerged until the trust was re-established. The heavy veil of not knowing what on earth was happening to us gradually lifted until the whole group could perceive that it had been through a process of self-discovery. Through uncovering all that was painful or joyful within us we had begun to see each other so that the group now saw itself. This unleashed new levels of relaxed camaraderie and togetherness.

This passage during the winter of 2002 was a turning point. As our long retreat progressed we still encountered plenty of challenges as a group but we had learned something about how to deal with our difficulties. We had learned to trust in the process of sitting together, deeply listening to each other and allowing chaos to emerge until order, harmony and resolution returned.

I also distinctly remember a day when we were coming out of our small temple after performing a daily *puja* (group ritual) to discover the entire house filled with a dense smoke. Tiny flakes of fat covered everything – the windows, the tables, the walls and the ceiling. A kettle full of palm oil that had been melting to fill our lamps had been left on the hob by one of our lackadaisical brothers and it had boiled over and burnt, filling the whole place with an acrid smelling film of burnt fat. We withdrew to the yoga room, one of the few places left untouched, where we could breathe and get into a group discussion about how to clean up our home and make sure everyone had a place to sleep.

Once again we went through that familiar process of diverse opinions, recriminations, polarised strategising and the heavy weight of not knowing how we would pull together to sort things out. It felt as if we were a fifteen-headed beast wanting to pull in fifteen different directions!

But we were also in a crisis and so we stuck together, committed to finding a common plan of action; and it did emerge. From the quagmire of not having one clear direction to follow, a new suggestion eventually arose that stopped everyone in their tracks because it had woven together previously diverse ideas into a new synthesis that struck us all in unison as being the answer. No one felt left out. To be honest I don't remember exactly what that plan of action consisted of but I do recall the sense of shared elation as collective knowing suddenly arose out of confusion. A mutually experienced and palpable sense of direction and unity filled our yoga room. Beaming smiles lit up our faces as we got up and prepared to get to work cleaning up our *drupkhang* (retreat house.) Despite the vexation of having a smelly and soiled house there was also a sense of joy in the meeting of minds and the 'all hands on deck' feeling of working together with the same intent and purpose.

I lived in the Buddhist monastery from 1998 until 2007 and whilst I was there I learned a great deal about meditation, Tibetan ritual and culture, and my own personal limitations and qualities. In general, Buddhist institutions are arranged as hierarchies of power and decision-making. However in my three years of group retreat we had to come to decisions in a more horizontal fashion and two learnings from this time stand out as particularly relevant to the work in which I'm now engaged. First, any 'mandala', group, society or living system functions optimally when every constituent part or member actively participates. I noticed in retreat that any time I withheld my opinions or perspectives through my tendency to be reserved I was in fact doing everyone a disservice. Conversely, when I got over my prolonged reticence and spoke up it often contributed to important shifts in the group dynamics. Second, when you have a group with a high level of participation you inevitably face moments of tension and conflict because of diverging perspectives and this leads to moments of confusion, inertia and turbulence. These brief or enduring moments are periods of collective not-knowing which hold great importance. For it is from this not-knowing that new perspectives of a synergistic elegance and beauty can arise if the group is able to trust, continue in its process and hold this uncomfortable tension.

¡Tengo la Solución!

These days I'm no longer a Buddhist monastic. Feeling cut off from society at large and desiring to reacquaint myself with aspects of life such as work and relationships, I gave back my vows and returned to my home town of London in 2009 to start life afresh. It was no easy transition. In my last years of monastic life I had started to become interested in Western psychotherapy and upon returning to mainstream society it became more a necessity for my survival than a mere interest. It was as if so much of me had been exiled during this period of spiritual quest that those aspects of my being required for life in the outside world needed to be re-owned and reintegrated. I discovered the theories of sub-personalities and shadow work and started to train in a method called Voice Dialogue which I still practise to this day. I came to understand and appreciate that even within an individual all the diverse inner aspects need to contribute and be heard if one's life is to be balanced and functional. My therapeutic work gradually reawakened aspects of my life and personality that had existed before my monastic experience and, informed by this notion of the necessity of having every voice heard and respected, I re-embarked on an interest in social activism.

*

It was 2011. The world was in a state of social discontent, starting with the Arab Spring, moving on through mass protests in Spain and elsewhere in mainland Europe, and on to the USA and the UK with the Occupy movements. Having seen videos of the mass popular assemblies taking place in public squares in Spain and inspired by the way these were more than just protests but forums for citizens' debate and collective deliberation, I decided to visit the *indignados* (as they were known) outside the Spanish Embassy in London. What I saw there inspired me massively: young, intelligent and engaged individuals, many of them economic migrants, sitting down together, taking their time and discussing their collective predicament. Fortunately understanding their Spanish I could appreciate that they were trying to work out what to do next and how to expand their movement. The day I first visited them they were grappling with some difficult questions concerning the identity of their movement. The group was getting restless: conflicting ideas were bandied around as the evening was setting in. Then suddenly one woman got up excitedly, walked around the assembled people and shouted, "Tengo la solución!" She explained her idea and what I witnessed next was of the very same order as the moments in retreat when we had collectively 'cracked it'. She had come up with a new solution that had integrated the diverging viewpoints that had preceded it. It was not so much her own idea but a culmination of the group process – all the effort and stuckness and dogged determination of the participants in crossing the desert of their not-knowing. The joy spread out through the assembly. I was genuinely moved, as I looked around the group of thirty to forty Spaniards, that everyone seemed happy at finding an answer to this issue of how to further their campaign. The assembly was adjourned and contented voices dispersed into the summer evening. I felt I had tasted something extremely significant in my questioning of how human society could work differently.

The inspiration of what I'd seen in retreat and then in activist circles led me to learning and experimenting with various group facilitation modalities that I now work with. These days I can state with conviction that our collective not-knowing is every bit as important as our collective knowing. The latter cannot arise without deep immersion in the former. Theories around the way human gatherings can bear fruit have dramatically changed. A current keyword is 'emergence' and this requires a very new, yet ancient, collective skill set. This new/ancient wisdom sees every participant in a group or society as being a unique sensor of the whole system. As systems thinker Peter Senge says: "You need to get different people, from different points of view, who are seeing different parts of the system to come together and collectively start to see something that individually none of them see."

Facilitators who are well-versed in emergent group process refer to the period in which a group goes through the collective unknowing as the 'groan zone' or the 'yuck stage'. So what exactly is happening there? And why is this stage of not-knowing so important?

Current thinking in coaching and facilitation sees that, when a group of people is working on a problem together, what tends to arise first in the discussion is everything the group already knows. This is the stage in which all of our habitual concepts and frameworks regarding a problem or situation are 'purged' or 'downloaded'. This is the stage in which we all tend to repeat the opinions and judgements we already know; and the facilitator's job is simply to get all this out and in the open. This phase of discussion tends to be relatively comfortable, although conflicting perspectives may arise. If the process used for the meeting is not an emergent one, then the different views are likely to be laid out, then perhaps voted upon, with one idea coming out on top whilst other suggestions may be discarded. In other words, the discussion is curtailed at this stage. This approach typifies our current paradigm of meetings and democratic procedures and is founded upon a deep-seated aversion to not-knowing.

What follows, once all of the existing information held by the group is purged, and if group members are committed to carry on working on an issue together, is a feeling of 'how can we ever reconcile all of this divergent and seemingly conflicting information?'. This is the groan zone and the point at which the discussion enters the frustration, and the profundity, of not-knowing. Previously held ideas have been exhausted and, in the absence of voting for a winning idea, no single proposition can triumph. So, in order to make progress, the participants now have to become creative. In this phase, even if participants are visibly exasperated, the facilitator trusts in their process and refrains from steering them in any direction. Uncomfortable silences are embraced even if they feel eternal. It is as if the collective vessel has been emptied so that something new can emerge. This period of not-knowing corresponds to the zero point, a vacuum, the Buddhist concept of *sunyata* (emptiness), the unborn, the root of all things.

This stage of not-knowing is important to humanity to the extent that it is coupled with a desire for its opposite: knowing. This polarity or kinesis produces an energy which we experience as discomfort, restlessness or a frustrating lack of productivity. So, there is to some extent a right attitude to adopt vis-à-vis this stage if we wish to use it constructively. For example, if we didn't have a desire to know how to proceed collectively we would simply arrive at the stage of not-knowing and say, "We don't know what to do – let's go home!" The other extreme (which is how our democratic systems tend to work) is to avoid or suppress this discomfort by settling for win/lose solutions that satisfy a few but not the totality. Holistic facilitation practice sees the energy created between the poles of not-knowing and desiring to know as being inherently generative.

Holding the group in the state of paradox and continuing the process of deliberation is the creative tension that gives birth to new ideas. The energy has to go somewhere. If the holding space doesn't feel safe or the process re-polarises into recriminations, the energy becomes destructive. Yet, with all the right conditions in place, this energy of not-knowing becomes almost magically creative. The polarity creates a 'third entity' – in this case a new and collectively owned solution to a problem. The trust in which a facilitator using emergent process holds a discussion is one of knowing that the group has an ability to self-organise. Just as an acorn has the self-organising potential to grow into an oak tree given the right conditions, so the facilitator has to provide a conducive atmosphere in which the group can self-organise in the desert of conflicting views and not-knowing.

Bogged Down in Devon

A couple of years ago I was invited, along with a colleague, to facilitate an emergent discussion around the question of "How Can We Improve Well-Being for the People of Totnes?" We were thrilled and full of expectation for the people in this progressive Devon town. Several prominent individuals from the local area involved in social change were going to be joining 20 or so others. We had four hours allocated for the discussion. The participants arrived, we explained how we would facilitate and the discussions began. The experience, however, proved to be a much more epic task than we had anticipated. The exploration of such a broad and labyrinthine subject as well-being meant the entire allotted time was spent diverging outwards into complexity. Each participant had their own take on what improving well-being meant, ranging from the political and systemic to ideas for community cafés and physical exercise groups. Before we knew it, our time together was over and the whole group was left hanging in the unknowing mess of the yuck stage. No clear way forward for improving well-being had emerged. Closing the process at this stage felt heavy and as the participants left both my colleague and I sensed the frustration in the lack of resolution.

That evening I wrote an email to my facilitation mentor explaining my disheartened feelings regarding the afternoon's discussions. Interestingly, she responded by saying not to worry and simply to write up the harvested notes and do some sorting so that the diverse array of ideas could be arranged according to the salient topics that had emerged. On returning to London after the weekend in Devon I got to work doing just that and as I typed out the notes I was amazed to see patterns emerging, and a deep level of reflection that truly embraced the complexity of this question. It was as if I was recording a snapshot of the collective not-knowing state they had reached. Doing this light untangling work revealed and unpacked just how much work the group had in fact done. That evening I sent the notes to the convener who had invited us. I was delighted when he responded saying how impressed they were with the clarity of the content and how it would be important as a basis for further work. For me this was further proof that, even when a discussion reaches a turbulent stage of intractable confusion, there is nevertheless something vital taking place.

A Future of Ancient Community Wisdom?

Our Western culture tends to package human meetings and gatherings into the confines of neatly arranged time limits. For us, time is primary; whereas ancient peoples and cultures were much more fluid in their relationship with time. Anthropologists have noted for example that Aboriginal peoples do not perceive time as an exclusively 'linear' category, giving at least equal weight to it as an eternal quality. Indeed, indigenous tribes such as the Native Americans have held, and still do hold, 'council' in circles that are convened and last for days as they traverse their deserts of not-knowing, and listen and discuss for as long as necessary until the group wisdom emerges to give responses that satisfy the whole. Such peoples know human deliberation and creativity to be an organic process with its own laws and logic that cannot be subjected to manipulation or control. In concrete terms this means meetings held according to these principles require time and patience. When there is a strong sense of community, humans perceive the necessity of evoking collective wisdom as a priority. We can afford to take the time to negotiate the uncomfortable passage of not-knowing. In a profit-focused society such as ours we end up caught in short-sighted thinking, believing we simply cannot spend too much time in not-knowing, which is perceived as dithering and a lack of dynamism. The result of this is inappropriate action, misaligned to the realities of our problems and short-termism that 'kicks the can down the road' rather than addressing the root causes of our malaise.

Creating space for discussion where there is no control over outcomes and being willing to let a group stew in not-knowingness is a courageous endeavour. However, an increasing number of businesses and community organisations are coming to understand the value of this approach. In November 2013, I travelled to the Austrian state of Vorarlberg to learn from practitioners who had helped establish Citizens' Wisdom Councils there with randomly selected citizens coming together to discuss important local issues. The idea was not to create a debate or end up voting but to do the deep transformational work of evoking new collective choices that embrace diversity and complexity. The initiative had been so successful that these participatory councils ended up being enshrined in the state constitution. I heard many stories of how the citizens would often start out complaining about the state of things and blaming others. Then, as they continued talking over a day and a half, they let go of what they 'knew' and gradually realised that the issues did not just concern government or businesses but that they, the citizens themselves, had a real role to play. The councils would often finish in the same states of joy and togetherness that I had witnessed in retreat or with the Spanish activists. In Bregenz, Austria, there is a famous example of one such council in which in locals were at loggerheads with town planners wanting to build an underpass beneath a railway near the lakeside. After a day and a half of difficult discussions a new plan emerged, satisfying both the locals and the planners, to build an attractive bridge that would be a feature for the whole town. Having gone through the travails of their collective deliberation over the weekend, the citizens, who previously didn't know each other, now experienced such a degree of shared enthusiasm that they stayed behind in their remaining free time to build a model of the bridge they had envisioned.

I feel that these are the kinds of outcomes that are the promise of spaces where diverse people can be held in the tension of their differences. I've seen time and again how a group simmering in the crucible of collective not-knowing, whilst remaining connected, is a generative and positive state. It bears fruit when held with skilful care and attention. Given the crises humanity faces as we struggle to ensure a sustainable future, I would like to see the creation of all kinds of forums where we can embrace our shared not-knowing and celebrate its potential. The joy of the successful meeting of minds that I witnessed in retreat, outside the Spanish Embassy and in working with community groups is something that can be replicated everywhere. It is my conviction that we are entering a stage of our evolution in which we are just starting to appreciate once again, the importance of collective intelligence, the hive-mind and the wisdom of crowds. Such intelligence and wisdom is a deeper knowing than the level of individualised rationality that our atomised culture presently relies on. Its very emergence is predicated upon not-knowing. Perhaps our multiple planetary crises will force us to abandon our hyper-individualistic ways and bring the multiplicity of ideologies, cultures and creeds together to hammer out diverging viewpoints in spaces of not-knowing. Whether this is achievable or not – well, we just don't know. But in convening these spaces, I for one feel called to try!

The Dance of Knowing and Not-Knowing in Herbal Medicine

Owen Okie

Not-knowing inculcates itself into every facet of herbal medicine: as a stance of openness, a check against assumptions or fixed and limited perspectives, a grounded state in the turbulence of complex interrelated perspectives, a holding of space for the client's unfolding potential, a starting point for the exploration of medicinal plants, and as a fundamental spiritual experience/dimension within which nature incessantly dances.

> *On the first day of the clinical phase of my MSc in Herbal Medicine I walk down the corridor beside my first client toward the consulting room. I know nothing about him, except his name and the obvious fact that he is African. I spent my toddler years in West Africa and I find that helps ground my jitters. Sitting down, we dive into the process of filling this lack of knowledge with as much information as possible. At this stage, not-knowing, in the sense of lacking information, is the starting point and the task that must be addressed.*

I am going to explore the dance of knowing and not-knowing that takes place within my life-role as a herbalist. A great deal of knowledge – both information and skills – is required in herbal medicine: knowledge of Western and Eastern models of physiology and pathology, of pharmacology, botany, phytochemistry, *materia medica*, drug-herb interactions, treatment approaches, and so on. There are at least two types of knowing involved: the epistemic knowledge of information and facts, and the embodied and holistic knowing that we might term 'gnosis'. We will look at the necessity and limitations of these two types of knowing within the realms of science and herbal medicine. The stance of not-knowing is a vital check on the potential pitfalls of knowing (or thinking one knows), including the tipping over of knowing into belief.

Not-knowing certainly plays an important role in the consultation room. An openness to new information and impressions is vital when working with a client – in both the assessment phase and the monitoring of progress. Considerable harm occurs through defining individuals by a diagnosis (client as disease) or by a constitutional typology (client as type). The not-knowing stance avoids the danger of making assumptions about the client or the condition. It protects us from the common error of forcing a client (and their symptoms, story and physiological data) towards our own preconceived conclusion, which can often blind us to the true root of their dis-ease and thereby the path to their healing.

As a herbalist, not-knowing even has 'spiritual' implications. When I am opened to a sense of wonder – through the study of the intricacies of human physiology or the contemplation of the complex interactions of plants within their ecosystems – I am invited into relationship with mystery, and into an embodied experience of the vast complexity and creativity that can never be fully grasped by the rational mind. This is a call to let go of my limited knowing, to fall into a state of observing, experiencing, sensing and feeling without the constant discrimination and limitations of normal cognition. Such a moment of not-knowing grounds me in a more fundamental way of being. When I emerge, and see a plant or my client before me, I know again that they can never be fully known by me, that they too rest within this vast, imponderable dimension.

When I first see a client I often know nothing about him except his name and the sound of his voice. This is the best place to start: knowing next to nothing. Two hours later I will have several detailed pages of notes. Yet how much do I really know about him even then? I know only what he's shared with me and what my intuition may have presented to me: his sleep and emotional patterns, dietary habits, childhood history, a bit about his family, his aches, pains, and irritations; his behaviour and the glimmers I can get from interviewing him, observing him, and taking his pulse; along with a sense of his presence, how it feels to be around him.

> *The first question I ask my first client is: "What brought you in today to see a herbalist?" He answers: weight, digestive discomfort, low energy/fatigue and foot pain. Then begins a fairly systematic process of trying to uncover the emotional, mental and physiological patterns of this individual's constitution and what lies behind his presenting symptoms. During this process a narrative begins to unfold that leads to an assessment – held lightly – of why my client is experiencing his difficulties. This may involve the 'trying on' of different perspectives or lenses, perhaps including different models of understanding human*

> *health and disease such as Western physiology or traditional Chinese medicine. By bringing into focus certain themes of the narrative, such lenses can reveal the obstructions and disharmonies within the system and what approach will provide the best leverage for effecting change. Conversely, these lenses might obscure or ignore potentially important factors. In this case it is apparent that my client's irregular night-shifts are creating a large burden on his system and resulting in low energy, poor sleep quality, disrupted circadian rhythm, and difficulty regulating blood sugar. Insufficient exercise (in part due to his foot pain) and some dietary factors are additional contributors. I come up with recommendations and discuss them with the client before we form a strategy incorporating lifestyle and nutritional modifications. He then heads down to the apothecary to get his formulas filled out.*
>
> *We are stepping back into the realm of not-knowing. Any changes he makes or herbs he takes will be as rocks thrown into a pond. We shall see how they alter the complex and dynamic patterns of ripples of his mind-body-spirit and whether that leads towards a more harmonious and vital interplay.*

The difficulty in putting all this into words, of course, is that not-knowing is not definable; it is of the realm of the unmanifest, of what Buddhists call *sunyata* (meaning both emptiness and infinite potentiality). Anything I say can only be an aspect or a facet of the object of description. Even saying that is inherently misleading for only the manifest realm can have aspects and facets. Such terms refer to knowable phenomena. Not-knowing slips between the cracks of all objects, phenomena, descriptions and experiences. It is outside the bounds of our day-to-day senses. I can only circumambulate 'it' – this 'it' which is everything and nothing – though 'it' also has no circumference!

So, in order to explore the many ineffable dimensions of not-knowing some contrast with knowing may be useful. Both epistemic and gnostic ways of knowing rest within the limitations of perspective. Knowing is bound within its own native perspective(s); and the validity of knowing, of either kind, becomes suspect when it oversteps those perspectival boundaries. This overstepping is one way to differentiate between knowing and belief. A belief is a statement of supposed knowing that has potentially lost track of, or overreached, its bounds and its realm of validity. Avoiding this pitfall, so tempting to the human mind, requires an acceptance of not-knowing – specifically the not-knowing of a subject from every possible perspective. We can explore this in a more concrete way, using the example of science.

As a herbalist I lean heavily upon the knowledge and understanding of science. Scientific understanding of human physiology, sociology, evolution and ecology in health and disease provide invaluable leverage for alleviating suffering and catalysing positive change and transformation. When science is coherently interwoven with traditional medicine, Eastern medical models, the wisdom traditions, psychotherapy, and so on, we get a synergistic approach that is far greater than the sum of its parts. The first step, however, is to understand the limitations and blind-spots (as well as the strengths) of each perspective/methodology.

Science is today often considered the greatest and, by some, *only* valid route to knowing truth and reality. It is understood as a method which consists of observation, measurement and experimentation; of the development of hypotheses followed by their testing and correction. Scientific methodology is aimed at minimising the subjective biases of the researchers in the hope of approaching a theoretically objective reality. Nevertheless beliefs and assumptions do filter through into the interpretation of observations resulting in biases and hypotheses which no longer hold up under rigorous experimentation. It is human nature to observe that which reinforces our pre-existing beliefs (an insight well described by Buddhist psychology and known to research theory as *confirmation bias*), and, moreover, to defend that belief in spite of evidence to the contrary. When this occurs we enter the realm of beliefs which need not rest upon testable facts.

Fortunately science is generally self-correcting and over time theories-turned-beliefs are challenged, re-tested in different ways and overthrown, or simply adjusted to better match the current 'state of knowledge'. Part of this process involves sorting out the 'science' from the 'myth' of any given system of knowledge – be that Western physiology, Ayurvedic medicine, or traditional Ojibwa herbalism.

Perspectivism remains key in understanding this process. Science, from its earliest beginnings, has favoured a limited number of perspectives in its attempts to describe the world. Each of these – e.g. empirical science or systems theory – readily falls into the trap of believing its perspective is the only valid one. Ken Wilber's Integral Theory[1] aptly describes this as an "absolutism". The counter-position is that scientific understanding is merely *part* of the truth – or one way of looking at it. One corrective to

---

[1] Ken Wilber is a prolific transpersonal theorist who has sought to integrate bodies of knowledge and types of knowing.

absolutism of any kind is a stance of not-knowing. By this I again mean the cultivation of open curiosity towards phenomena, towards one's own and others' experiences, a constant questioning and suspension of assumptions, hypotheses and theories, a willingness to see the world through other eyes, through different worldviews, perspectives, value systems, philosophical and cultural viewpoints, and so on: in short, an embodied realisation that no one can hold the complete and only truth, that all truths are partial and that ultimately one *cannot* know in an absolute and final sense.

> *Studying for my MSc in Herbal Medicine I experience great moments of insight as I see how two seemingly incompatible ways of knowing all of a sudden correlate despite looking at the same situation from very different angles. As my professor lectures about the pathophysiology of liver disease and the role and impact of inflammation, I suddenly align this with my understanding of physiology from the perspective of Chinese medicine – liver 'fire', excess yang, deficient yin, etc. The patterns found clear in Chinese medicine between the liver and the eyes (in jaundice, the whites of the eyes often become yellow) and between the liver and emotions such as anger and depression (the liver plays a significant role in our emotional states due to its metabolism of our hormones: liver 'fire' rising is associated in Chinese medicine with what we call menopausal symptoms such as hot flushes) become clear.*

Despite these moments of insight I had no way of systematically locating these various ways of understanding and ultimately co-ordinating them to maximise their healing potential. This is where Integral Theory is an invaluable tool, particularly in the forms of AQAL and Integral Methodological Pluralism.[2]

---

[2] Unpacking Integral Theory is beyond the scope of this article. AQAL stands for All Quadrants, All Levels, Lines, States, and Types. These five elements give us the minimal framework for integrally (fully and holistically) understanding any given phenomenon. AQAL applies itself very naturally to herbal medicine and health as a way of ensuring you do not miss important information/perspectives vis-à-vis your client. Any of Wilber's books since *Sex, Ecology, Spirituality* will introduce AQAL. Integral Methodological Pluralism is described as a set of behavioural injunctions/practices that bring about a set or range of enacted experiences and is composed of three principles: non-exclusion, enfoldment and enactment. IMP is a valuable tool for locating and coordinating perspectives. See Wilber's *Integral Spirituality.* For the specific application of Integral Theory to health and herbal medicine, see my blog and resource page: www.integralherbalism.wordpress.com

I have shown some of the ways in which not-knowing plays an important role in herbal medicine. My professor, James Snow, told us, "Every time the client comes in for a follow-up, meet them for the first time". Preserving that stance of receptiveness, not having the client and his problems definitively pinned down, allows for new information and insight to emerge in each encounter, and again avoids writing off the client as a walking pathology ("Here comes Mr. Ulcerative Colitis") or as a constitutional/personality type ("Here comes Mr Pitta with a little Vata; he's the definition of Type A").

There is a paradoxical relationship between the client's describable, and seemingly fixed, qualities and quantities, on the one hand, and his creative potential for healing (or 'wholing'), growth and transformation, on the other. As a herbalist I have to remain open to both sides of that paradox.

> *The principle of not-knowing is put into play when my client returns for his first follow-up two weeks later. What has changed? Has anything changed? Is he miraculously 'healed'? Am I a brilliant herbalist? We sit down. Still tired, foot still hurting... And the digestion? He waves his hand dismissively: "No problem". Years of painful bloating are now consigned to the past, forgotten, and we delve with more detail into sleep, exercise, diet and strategies for improving the pain.*

According to Zen Master Dōgen and his idea of being-time (*uji*), my client is rising and falling from the unmanifest realm of infinite possibility (*sunyata*) in every moment. Like all organisms he is an infinitely complex dance of interdependent co-arising conditions (also known in Buddhism as dependent origination). Trapped in his conditioning, habit-patterns (*samskaras*) and identity-building, he is also, again paradoxically, in each moment liberated, full of creative potential and freedom of choice. These *samskaras* are themselves concretised and codified 'knowings', beliefs and attitudes formulated in the client's experience and world-view. His values, constitutional type and cultural and karmic heritage precipitate and take shape as mental formations and emotional weather patterns which further solidify into physiological and metabolic patterns and anatomical structures.

Therefore, my role as herbalist is largely that of an educator, or more often a re-educator, supporting the client in freeing himself, as mind-body-spirit, from such entrenched patterns of so-called knowing, and opening to the possibility of healthier, more adaptive patterns of being and doing. A healthy stance towards life necessitates a certain degree of not-knowing, a freedom to have new responses to what arises in every moment. I seek to model this when I am with him. This understanding is also one of the aims and gifts of meditation. Automatically reacting to new circumstances with old patterns will effect no change. Resilient individuals maintain flexibility in their mental, emotional and behavioural responses.

For my part, I do my best not to remain stuck in my attitudes and to facilitate a similar stance in my client. To sit in not-knowing is a state of being: open to, and supportive of, another's creative potential, his ability to liberate himself from the rigid patterns and assumed identities and to change, heal, grow and transform.

The client is also often blind to, and hiding from, various aspects of himself. In psychotherapeutic circles we would talk of his shadow, those rejected and repressed elements that we are only minimally, if at all, aware of, that we have relegated to the dark realm of the unknown. The exploration of the shadow is often a necessary stage in the client's healing; and it may require great courage for him to face and enter this place. He usually has both superficial unknowns – places that with a little questioning he will quickly become aware of – and deeper and darker unknowns that will require far more thorough and arduous exploration.

> *I am on my third consultation with my first ever client when I finally discover the deeper motivation for his coming to see me, the one that actually has enough emotional energy behind it to initiate change. His digestive discomfort is resolved, his foot greatly improved. His remaining stated concerns are to lose weight, lower his blood pressure and increase his energy. These motivators are apparently insufficient to get him to eat better and exercise more (as also suggested by his doctor), or to get more sleep. He is a sharp and educated man, he understands very well the reasoning behind my recommendations, but he has yet to make any significant changes. At the end of the third visit he says, "My girlfriend is coming to visit in a few weeks and I'm having trouble maintaining an erection..."*

Once the physiological and behavioural patterns have been elucidated, the real mystery, the stories and motivations of the deep interior, can be explored. As a herbalist the greatest challenge is *not* figuring out which botanical, nutritional and lifestyle recommendations will help a client but actually getting the client to follow through and implement the changes. Usually he comes with a pretty good idea of what he needs (most clients know they should exercise more and eat better). What he needs from me is an exploration of how and why he got stuck in his current ruts, and why he is often caught somewhere between wanting to, and feeling unable to, change. This is again where herbal medicine crosses into the territory of the psychotherapist. Traumas long past, sexual, physical and psychological abuse, deeply buried issues around body-image and food, bad experiences in gym class, codified attitudes ("exercise should not be fun") – all these may create hidden obstacles preventing the client from acting on his best intentions.

Several months later, at another follow-up, I discover my client has purchased (and is using) an indoor bike, has managed to change onto a regular daytime work schedule, and has long since finished his supply of herbs. His sexual problem has also resolved itself. For him, loss of sexual capacity was a warning sign about lack of self-care.

However, eight months later he returns with the same problem: "My girlfriend is coming to visit..." After some investigation I discover that he is now day trading online, which requires him to get up for a couple of hours in the middle of the night. Loss of sleep and disruption of circadian rhythm result in fatigue, low energy, blood sugar deregulation and a return of the erectile dysfunction.

Samskaras (habit-patterns) are again at play here. The client has fallen back into his old rut, apparently without even realising it. How often, I wonder, must life teach us variations of the same lesson before we move from a superficial and temporary fix to a deeper transformation and healing?

But I am not immune from such patterns and blindspots myself. For me, as an addicted and compulsive learner, not-knowing can serve as a kind of cattle-prod. If only I knew! If only I knew, *thoroughly*, Tibetan medicine, Chinese medicine, Ayurvedic medicine, integrative physiology, Buddhist psychology; if only I had mastered pulse-reading and could predict a client's potential for pathology ten years down the line; if only I knew the thousands upon thousands of plants and foods in the worldwide repertoire of medicinal substances, and their phytopharmacology, and, and... Not-knowing is, in this context, a vital reminder: I don't, and can't, know it all (and would be insufferable if I did). My knowing is riddled with holes and cracks of various sizes; in different realms it dwells in various degrees of shallowness and depth; but it is never complete.

Dwelling in not-knowing also provides room for the intuitive faculties to present insights that may lie outside the purview of formalised knowledge.

My not-knowing also represents a trust in the inherent knowing of the client; and provides space for the arising of insight and embodied knowledge in him and in the therapeutic space between us. Maybe it delineates, or facilitates, a vital difference between a knowledgeable and competent expertise in the treatment room and a more fluid, dynamic and embodied gnosis, opening into a compassionate and inspired presence.

I certainly do not discount the 'expertise' my training has conferred. But even here, and specifically in the realm of the senses, not-knowing is an excellent guide in the exploration of our wild, potentially medicinal, plants, the fundamental material of my work. Clearly, if you go into a new forest on a new continent and eat a plant or mushroom because it looks familiar from home you could be in for an unpleasant surprise. Thinking you know more than you do can sometimes be physically dangerous.

> *We have seen how not-knowing is a valuable stance before a client.*
>
> *Similarly, as a forager entering a new domain, not-knowing is the starting place. In my wanderings I happen upon an intriguing plant. I sit with it and calm my mind. I explore it with all my senses: sight, touch, smell and finally taste. The tiniest touch of my tongue to the jagged edge of a ripped leaf. A burst of bitterness. I attend to the tastes and wait. Wait. Sometimes I get a noticeable felt-sense, a shift in my physical and emotional body. Then I might chew and spit out a small piece of leaf. A slight astringency in the mouth. Wait.*

It is in part by exploring the six tastes (sweet, sour, salty, bitter, pungent and astringent) that humans have learnt and come to understand the medicinal nature of plants. In Chinese, Ayurvedic and Tibetan medicine the taste of the plant is indicative of its medicinal effects. This is often borne out by modern pharmacology and the study of plant chemistry. This exploration of a plant via the human senses is known as *organoleptic testing*.

This is where the spiritual dimension opens up again: as a phenomenological being, often a *being-with*. This may be a being with a plant, a being with a client, a being with nature, a being with mystery. The bits and pieces, the frameworks and the meta-frameworks of my knowledge once more drop away and what is left is the empty space within which all manifests. Not-knowing *becomes* knowing or perhaps *now*-ing. For just that moment. And then I'm back, kneeling before the plant with my *hori-hori*, my Japanese knife, in my hands, digging up a root. I smile and, having tasted it – in the fullest sense – I place it in my cloth wild-crafting bag, before opening myself to sense the next plant ready for harvest.

To sacrifice is to make sacred and in this ceremony, reaching back through thousands of generations of human and even non-human ancestors, this plant's life has been made sacred. I know nothing of the future client who will benefit from this plant I have so carefully gathered. Several years may pass before a client presents with a symptom pattern perfectly matching the medicinal qualities of the root.

So, after a consultation, how *does* one select a specific plant for a unique individual and his condition? Western medicine as currently practised usually resorts to trial and error, but Tibetan and Ayurvedic medicine are far more specific in matching person to remedy. In fact taste is again one of the guiding principles. The taste of the plant reveals its composition, and this is matched to the individual's constitution and condition. For example, if an individual is experiencing excess fire (heat, redness, inflammation, anger), he will be provided with a cooling remedy (such as a bitter-tasting plant) along with a moistening remedy such as liquorice, which is sweet and anti-inflammatory.

Each plant contains thousands of phytochemicals, *secondary metabolites*, which play roles in the internal communications of the plant itself as well as its external communications with other plants in its community, and in the plant's immune function, or else manifest as aromatic oils that ward off insects. The life-force, vitality, innate intelligence, or, in Ayurvedic terms, *prana*, of the root I harvest will, upon ingestion, also have a message for the physiology and metabolism (in body-mind-spirit) of the client. The compounds will be smelled and tasted and will send signals to the central nervous system and down to the body. The compounds will be digested, assimilated, and then metabolised, used and/or excreted. In the process they will interact with, speak to, alter and sometimes penetrate every tissue and every cell in the body that is open to their particular mode of communication.

In this interaction the sacred marriage between human and plant is consummated; as is that between the expert's knowledge and not-knowing.

> *I have seen my first client for the final time. Has he now truly learned and taken on board that his flagging libido was simply a warning about the need for self-care? Or might there be a yet deeper psychological puzzle, so far unrevealed, hiding underneath?*

I do not know.

An Ally in the Jungle:

Everything I Ever Wanted to Not-Know About Ayahuasca

Paul Christelis

Every man takes the limits of his own field of vision for the limits of the world

Arthur Schopenhauer

The motorboat carries provisions, barrels of drinking water, two Peruvian teenagers, our guide Brenda, my partner Pieter and me. We are headed away from Iquitos, a Peruvian outpost with no identifiable connection to the 21st century, ploughing through the expansive waters of the Amazon Basin towards Refugio Altiplano - *a paradise of natural healing and inspiration*, according to their website. The air is lush and humid, thick with butterflies and mosquitoes; the heat… Amazonian. The boat veers around a bend and we enter a stretch of water draped with curtains of foliage and a low-lying canopy of branches. This creates the illusion of a tunnel. As we motor through the dense thicket, a flashback: I'm sitting on the floor of my parents' bedroom, watching 'Apocalypse Now' on television. Coppola's Vietnam, exotic and electric, stuns and disturbs my fourteen-year-old sensibilities. I watch without understanding but the atmosphere lures me in. I turn to Pieter: 'Heart of Darkness', I whisper. But I think it gets lost beneath the clatter of the engine.

What are we doing here? There are a few possible explanations, which I present below, and then there is a different kind of response, an anti-explanation if you like, best summarised as follows: I don't know. But first, the explanations.

London, New Year's Eve. Pieter and I are watching Simon Amstell, the comedian, doing a stand-up show in which he talks about his experience drinking the indigenous plant medicine, ayahuasca (pronounced *eye-a-was-ka*). This takes place in a shamanic ceremony somewhere in the Amazon rainforest. Consciousness is expanded as a result of drinking it. The 'mother of all plant medicines' shows you what you need in order to heal and evolve. Something clicks for both of us. The next day we google *ayahuasca retreat amazon*, and a few days later book our flight to Peru.

The explanation goes further back, of course. My first memory of attempting to expand my consciousness is of a five- or six-year-old me in bed, in the dark, eyes screwed up tight, focusing on the black nothingness in front of me. For a reason I can't recall, I'm willing myself to sink ever deeper into the black, imagining that scrunching up my eyes will facilitate this. I discern that the black is not actually black, but rather a coca-cola brown (such are my reference points at this age) and this discovery spurs me on. The intensity ratchets up until I feel as if I'm falling backwards through space on an out-of-control rollercoaster. My body tenses, I grip the bed sheets. A mixture of encroaching fear and excitement - I'm experiencing something utterly new, self-made, unpredictable. My heart thumps in my ears, blood bristles. Then the thought: *Is this dying?*

I'm a happy child, often singing and drawing attention to myself, but sometimes, at night, I wake in fright, consumed by the awesome awareness that I will someday die. When this happens, I get out of bed and walk down the long, silent corridor into my parents' bedroom. There's the familiar scent of menthol and slumbering bodies, the tick of my father's alarm clock. I walk past his side of the bed and make my way towards my mother. Her smell is instantly soothing. She wakes when I tug her shoulder. "I'm scared of dying", I tell her, and she ushers me into bed with her where I'll stay until morning. This ritual plays itself out over the next year or so until death is relegated to a temporary latency. So it's somewhat surprising that I'm ostensibly attempting to manufacture a death experience through experimentation – if that's what I'm doing. I decide it's too risky to continue tumbling through inner space, and open my eyes.

Fallow years (in terms of mind expansion) proceed until I hit puberty. The big discovery, at fourteen, is masturbation. I throw myself into it with vigour, both excited and perplexed that the objects of my lust are my male friends. Consequently, I develop an underground, furtive sexuality whilst presenting myself on the outside as eligibly straight. Meanwhile, behind the bathroom door, I'm on the floor, school trousers around my ankles, inhaling Spray & Cook oven cleaner fumes to maximise the high of ejaculation. It's a bit like falling backwards on the rollercoaster, with the prospect of death replaced by the promise of bliss. My chemical adventures begin.

Fast forward to my twenties and I'm a respectable, middle class psychotherapist and budding novelist by day, a cannabis user at night. Smoking has become a habit and I'm long past the stage where the drug is providing useful insights. MDMA offers a few pleasurable peaks, but they are short-lived and the quality of the drug variable. It's LSD now that does the trick. I've moved from South Africa to London with my new partner, Pieter, and on the cusp of our thirties we've ditched our careers (he's an artist with a degree in fine arts), sold our possessions and gone bohemian. Armed with tabs of LSD, the Essential Writings of Krishnamurti and a dollop of earnestness, we trip our way through London, encountering art galleries, parks, shops and cinemas with minds sharpened and spirits reverberating. At a beach party in Cape Town, on a home visit, I have an astounding experience in which, by looking into the eyes of others, I'm able to see right through them into their emptiness, and by so doing allow them to recognise the emptiness themselves. And years later, in Iceland, tripping ecstatically through the alien, so-white-it's-blue landscape, I transcend my self and touch the translucent space of Not Me. I cry so much it feels as if my whole body is leaking tears. The tears are of sadness and joy, a perfect balance of the two – *sadjoy* - such that they too transcend themselves and dissolve into equanimity.

Perhaps this account gives the impression of drug fiends but in fact things are a lot more sober and mundane. The tripping is infrequent and for the most part meditation and reflection are the main ingredients of our diet. I read voraciously, the usual suspects: Burroughs, Leary, Osho, Hesse, Castaneda. It's Castaneda's texts detailing his shamanic apprenticeship with the Yaqui sorcerer, Don Juan, that really speak to me. Whether the writings are fact or fiction, there is something so cannily poetic, so intensely mysterious and searching about the world of sorcery that I'm determined to discover it for myself. And so, an opportunity presents itself.

For a year and a half I undertake a shamanic internship with an English shaman, Daniel, who I contact via a flyer on a notice board in a Camden bookshop. What catches my attention is his explanation of Inner Knowing that chimes with what I'm absorbing from Castaneda. "Our bodies hold all the knowledge that we need", says the flyer. "But our lives are so usually congested that we do not have the space to hear our own intelligence. When we give ourselves attention, we can make a Clear View... We can hear a voice that is in no doubt."

Ah, *a voice that is in no doubt*! I'm captivated by this prospect. My relationship with my voice is, literally, very much one of insecurity and doubt. As a schoolboy I have been both a public speaker, winning a regional competition and making it to the South African finals, as well as a sometimes-stutterer. I receive acclaim for playing the role of the great rhetorician, Mark Antony, in Shakespeare's *Julius Caesar*, and yet ask me to read aloud in class and I stumble over words that get caught in my throat. It's an odd irony that I don't quite register until years later. (Is the stutter my homosexuality in disguise, daring to speak its name, and then retreating?). And although this glitch has long since tapered off and I now speak fluently, the insecurity seems to be reconfiguring itself in the form of a pervading sense of stuckness that's beginning to define my London life: What am I doing here? Where am I going? Who am I? What began as a question is developing into a stutter. One winter's afternoon, watching a rollerblader gracefully gliding through Hyde Park, I realise that I'm not flowing, and it hurts.

Yearning to experience flow and grace I make an appointment and meet with Daniel. He's a few years older than me, bisexual, driven and focused. There's a bit of sexual tension between us but it's never addressed and I'm not sure it matters. Everything is Dream, he explains. The world is being dreamt, we are being dreamt. Our task is to listen to the dream. We do this by contacting the subtle energy body, the chakras, our animal guides. We cultivate multi-dimensional awareness by travelling inside, listening deeply and 'speaking the planet'. It all makes sense on paper but experientially I battle to integrate the concepts. I forge ahead, however, joining dreaming circles, being smudged with a smudge stick to clean my aura, meeting my spirit guides. (Do I really meet them, or is this just fanciful imagining?) But my shamanic journeying is timid and although I don't want to admit it, I'm out of my depth, or not on the right path, or just plain confused. Daniel's total dedication and unswerving belief in his life's work throws my confusion into sharp relief. I'm aimless, lost, a spiritual being in a gay man's body, marooned half way between hedonism and renunciation. One day I'm considering joining a monastery, the next I'm at a Radiohead gig. My relationship with my family becomes strained. They experience my leaving South Africa as a kind of rebellion and can't fathom why I'd throw away my career for a life waiting tables in restaurants for a pittance. Pieter's on his own trajectory, similar to mine in some ways, but flavoured by his own demons.

My work with Daniel ends. He moves to Mexico where he establishes a School of Dreaming. I give up the dream of shamanism, and continue my desultory wanderings.

During this turbulence, ayahuasca is nowhere on our radar. It's only years later that I become aware of it, and then only casually and sporadically. Simon Amstell's prompt, that New Year's Eve, isn't so much a rekindling of a flame as an unexpected call to arms that comes out of the blue. We hear his account, decide almost immediately to go to Peru and that's that. For four months we avidly research ayahuasca. We read books, articles, blogs, academic papers. We learn about plant shamanism from a number of disciplines – psychological, anthropological, biochemical, theosophical. YouTube offers a world of documentaries, both gonzo and conventional, and there is a seemingly never-ending stream of video diaries by seekers of all ages and cultures, filmed *in situ*, detailing experiences of drinking the medicine. Everyone has a unique reaction, running the gamut from mildly hallucinogenic to profoundly intense and life changing. Some are blessed with visions and insights of transcendental beauty, others are plunged into nightmarish realms and respond by screaming, wailing, begging for mercy. It all seems a little melodramatic to me, but then many of the diarists are young and earnest, as once was I (I'm now in my forties), and I imagine I might have over-reacted too at that age, desperate to conjure poetry and self-importance from every experience.

As I trawl through the literature I begin to wonder if I'd be better off not knowing all this stuff. I'm a psychotherapist and mindfulness teacher and if there's a cornerstone to my work it's to approach experience with fresh eyes, *beginner's mind*; to let go of what we think we know in order to discover what pulsates in the moment, whether that be in a therapy session, during meditation or while eating an orange. So why all this pre-production, this compulsion to absorb and digest before the event? It's because I'm curious, I tell myself, and that can only be a good thing. Along with not-knowing, curiosity is my stock-in-trade. It's permissible to arm myself with knowledge as long as it doesn't ossify into something *known*. In other words, I will bracket off what I learn about ayahuasca, hold it lightly in my awareness, and allow myself to forget it when I'm called upon to experience it myself.

*

...It's a perfectly reasonable explanation, the above. It fits neatly into my life's narrative, that ongoing drama I've spun from what would otherwise be an incoherent onslaught of things happening for no obvious purpose. Over the years I have fully invested in fashioning an identity for myself: *seeker, expander, healer*. Thus, I am able to know myself, my place in the world. I'm the container that gives shape to the onslaught of things happening.

But what if the container dissolves? What if my Amazonian quest is simply something happening that cannot be known by myself, by my limited narrative-bound awareness? The story goes: I embrace the unknown. But this unknown, being part of a story, has a shape. It's an ersatz unknown, nestling within the boundaries of my comfort zone.

What happens in the jungle will either solidify my story, or rip it to shreds.

*

Brenda is one a few Peruvian women hired by Refugio Altiplano to greet guests in Iquitos and bring them to the centre. She's attractive, impish and coyly enters into a harmlessly flirtatious relationship with us. She enjoys her job, which entails spending half her time in Iquitos and the other half at Refugio where she and the other staff basically hang around and look after guests' needs – accompanying them on forest walks, escorting them to nearby villages, acting as translators. These activities are all optional and secondary to the main event, the ayahuasca ceremonies. These take place at night, two nights on, one night off, meaning we will experience five ceremonies during our week here. Brenda's girlish disposition and penchant for Hello Kitty-esque accessories doesn't fit the image of the spiritual seeker. I ask her if she's tried ayahuasca. She screws up her nose in disgust: "Oh, no! I never touch it! It make you go...", and she makes a gushing gesture with her hands as if pushing some odious substance away from her face. She's referring to *la purga*, a common phenomenon during ceremony, and the one thing I'm not looking forward to: puking and possibly shitting myself. This makes both physiological and psychological sense to me: the body expelling a foreign substance as well as purging itself of accumulated psychic toxins. I like the idea of a psychological colonic, it's just the nausea and messiness I'd rather avoid. I'm with Brenda on this one but I hide my anxiety beneath cool bravado. Hey, I'm in the Amazon, boldly delving into mystery. How brave is that! How...manly.

We finally disembark at Refugio, a sprawling network of wooden houses and open-plan communal spaces all separated by large stretches of land. Labourers and chickens mill about in the unrelenting heat. Giggling Peruvian women wash clothes and cut vegetables in the shade.

Our house is a ten-minute walk from the main communal area where everyone meets for meals or to relax in one of the many hammocks. To get there, we follow a guide, a young Peruvian man in a washed-out T-shirt, a rifle slung over his shoulder. He silently leads us through an increasingly dense and dank undergrowth until we are completely engulfed in pure, primal forest. The gumboots we bought in Iquitos are essential – it's the rainy season and the mud is deep and thick. Essential too is the mosquito repellent, which we've lathered over exposed skin. The air sucks and nips at me; it hums with a giddy strangeness. As we continue to power through the forest, the hum stealthily escalates into a roar, swarming with the unseen, the unknown. Is that what the rifle is for? To shoot at the unknown? Should I begin to fear something?

Our house is a rotund, two-storey building hovering over the forest floor. From inside there are 360 degree views of imposing foliage, all shades of green - dark, fern, mantis, moss. The layers of verdancy play off each other like a hall of mirrors; scanning the environment is dizzying. I'm intoxicated by the otherness of it all and begin to count down the hours until the first ceremony, which is later tonight. We'll be fetched by a guide at around 7.30, and make our way by torchlight back to the communal area where we'll be deposited in the ceremonial hall (or 'the spaceship' as it's affectionately known) and wait for the fireworks to begin. But first, we will meet the head honcho, the owner of Refugio, the master shaman, Scott Petersen.

I already know something about Scott from my extensive web surfing. He's an American, an ex-business man and counsellor/anthropologist who relocated to the Amazon and underwent the gruelling, years-long training to become a shaman. From his blogs I can discern nothing vaguely spiritual or guru-esque about him. In fact he comes across as a bit of a cowboy, with his rootin', tootin' American drawl, grizzly features and the mischievous glint of someone who enjoys a stiff drink. Interestingly, this anti-image doesn't dissuade me from choosing him or Refugio Altiplano as my initiator. Not even the odd internet posting accusing him of taking advantage of lone female travellers puts me off. For the most part, at least according to TripAdvisor, Scott and his team behave immaculately, empathically and have facilitated ceremonies with great skill. All ratings of

Refugio are 5 star, with many visitors claiming that Scott is the finest shaman working with ayahuasca.

When we are taken to meet him later in the afternoon, once again accompanied by an armed guard, my first impressions remain largely confirmed, but in the flesh he radiates nuances accessible only to the fizz of an actual encounter. He is much smaller in person, although retaining a larger than life aura, bare-chested and immediately welcoming. "Hey brothers! Thanks for taking the trip to visit us." He embraces us and introduces Rachel, an American woman doing laundry. She's about my age, maybe younger, friendly and confident in that American way, but with a bruised quality in her eyes. There's a whiff of intimacy between her and Scott. A cursory scan of the room reveals a ruffled bed surrounded by dusty bottles and books, and a slew of garish psychedelic oil paintings positioned in every available free space. A laptop glows dimly on a sullied work surface, and next to it, nonchalantly lolling, is a hand gun. Any hint of disquiet is offset by his genuine friendliness and largesse. I trust him. Or, I want to trust him. I have no option but to trust him. There's no turning back.

Pieter and I take turns to meet with Scott, to discuss our intentions for this trip. I wait on the landing below while Pieter and Scott chat on his balcony, three storeys high, overlooking swathes of forest. Outside, the tree tops are swaying in the breath of an impending storm. It feels suitably ominous.

It's soon my turn to meet with Scott, and by now the rain has begun to fall in gloopy, heavy drops. Scott's still bare chested, swaying on his hammock while I sit beside him on a bench. I struggle to hear him over the hiss of the storm. He asks me what I've come for. "I want to work more deeply with my therapy clients", I say, feeling suddenly ultra-earnest. It's not the only intention I have, but it's the one that's easiest to articulate. I explain that I'm open to what ayahuasca has to teach me; "I'm ready to encounter the unknown". The more I talk, the more I want to retract. In this environment, with this man, this magnified, maximum-dose version of a man, my words sound feeble, pretentious. Scott is only twelve or so years older than me but in his presence I feel like a teenager. He continues to call me "brother" and although I do not doubt his willingness to foster between us a relationship based on equality, my insecurity wants to reject the fraternal in favour of the filial. I expect him to call me "son".

"What do I do with my intentions in the ceremony?", I ask . "Should I be aware of them or try to forget them and go in with no expectations?"

"Let it work subconsciously, brother. Don't try to guide it." He continues to mumble in a stream-of-consciousness manner, peppering his speech with detours into infectious laughter: "Hee, hee!" He actually does laugh like that – *hee, hee*! – as if a cartoon character or a caricature of a prankish schoolboy. It's endearing and comforting and somehow doesn't sit incongruously beside the gung-ho-ness and weaponry. I listen and try to absorb as much as possible, laughing with him even when I don't get what's funny. And then there are moments of absolute seriousness and resolve, and the mood shifts accordingly. He flits between states with a kind of mastery I've not seen before, as if his being is dancing, skipping. And all the while he is focused on me, not in an obvious I-am-listening-to-you-intently kind of way, but with a deceptive casualness.

Whiplashing rain is now making it impossible to hear anything, so we adjourn. Scott embraces me, a burly, enveloping hug. Beneath the cowboy veneer, the heart of an angel. An alluring contradiction. I feel I'm teetering on the edge of a precipice with Scott ensuring I won't fall off.

*

I'm ready to encounter the unknown. Am I actually aware of how platitudinous and bourgeois this sounds? Middle class psychotherapist has interest in mind expansion, hops on plane, drinks plant cocktail and *boom!* gives the Unknown a run for its money. The truth is, I can handle not-knowing in manageable doses. Being a psychotherapist facilitates this. For fifty minutes I am able to surrender to the mysteries of the client-therapist encounter, allowing myself to get swept up in the vortex of not understanding what is happening, straining here and there to make sense of it perhaps, but for the most part happy to hold my client's hand as we inch our way through the thicket. Post-session I write up a summary of the encounter, preserving some of the mystery but also translating it into a Known commodity with the aid of theory, prior experience, guesswork.

My client Max, who has been yearning for a romantic partner for years, finally meets a man who could be 'the one'. His name is Paul – same as mine. My immediate (internal) response in the session is to marvel at the co-incidence whilst also fleetingly considering the possible transference implications. But I allow these thoughts to dissolve into the Unknown. Afterwards, I write about it in a way that solidifies my response into a professional, considered appraisal of transference, drawing on my experience of supervision and previous meetings with Max. He has resisted intimacy with me for months; now, by opening himself to a Paul, he effectively (albeit it unconsciously) makes himself available for a deeper commitment to therapy, and to me. It makes neat, elegant sense. Not-knowing becomes potentially neutered by the Known[1].

Am I potentially neutering my ayahuasca experience?

*

So here it is, our first ceremony. The rain has dissolved and the night sky is awash with stars the size of plums. At 7.30pm a guard materialises outside our house, unobtrusively waiting to escort us to the ceremonial hut. It's dark already so we're completely reliant on him and the threads of light from our torches to lead the way. We stop off *en route* at another house and pick up a fellow participant, José, a young, buff ex-military man turned accountant. He lives in Los Angeles and is training to be an Integrated Energy therapist, healing with the energy of angels. I immediately warm to his gentle, wounded presence. Although our conversation is energetic and playful I detect an undertow of melancholy about him, an invisible fault line of battle-weariness. It's to be his very first ceremony too. He has no idea what to expect but he's hoping for a beautiful experience.

We arrive at the spaceship and prepare for lift-off. Mats are arranged in a circle in the belly of the cavernous space. We choose our spots and decamp – toilet roll, flashlights, water, puke bucket at the ready. There are a few other people here, most of whom we've briefly met, an assortment of seekers who are very serious about ayahuasca and a coterie of air stewards from Dubai who seem to be here for the thrill of it. At lunch (there's no dinner on a ceremony evening, ayahuasca requires an empty stomach) they share their experiences from the night before, comparing 'visions' and encounters. I listen politely but don't take any of it in – I want my own experience. Pieter, like me, senses the magnitude of what we're about to do, and shuts off contact with his chatty neighbours. We lie down and wait for Scott and the shamans to arrive. Gazing up into the rafters I spot a creature sitting on a beam, something resembling a giant rat but with a thicker tale. It perches for a time then darts across the beam and rests until another dash. I overhear some talk about the possibility of low flying bats and other creatures of the night infiltrating the hut.

A little later the two assistant shamans, both native Peruvians, arrive and take their place on either side of what I assume is Scott's seat. I'm not sure

---

[1] Or, if not by the Known, then by the Guessed At. But a guess can easily morph into a Known when the need to control and understand interferes.

what I was expecting but they don't conform to my fantasy of *ayahuasceros*. They look like labourers, which, I later discover, is what they are during the day. Such is the integration of the spiritual with the everyday in this part of the world. After some time, Scott arrives, followed by Rachel. It will transpire that she is a shaman-in-training, Scott's apprentice. She is also his lover. As they enter, an almighty rainstorm descends. Only moments ago the stars had been out, so where did this come from? A crack of lightning flashes the jungle with a petrifying light, a gauntlet thrown down by the spirit world. This is how it feels in the moment, which is as far removed from the gentrification of our neighbourhood in London as it's possible to be. Scott takes his position at the top of the circle, shirtless, in jeans and cowboy boots, looking as if he's about to wrestle a buffalo.

The ritual begins. Scott pours the dark syrupy liquid into a cup and drinks. The shamans come up and drink too. There are incantations and brief exchanges between them. Each group member will go up one at a time to drink. I'm third in line.

"I'm going to give you a little more than usual for a first ceremony because I want you to have a memorable experience." Scott pours a three-quarter cup and hands it to me. The gringo machismo is gone; he has shape-shifted into avuncular benevolence. I pause before drinking, eyes closed, marking the occasion. The liquid goes down easily and is almost pleasant-tasting, with a sharp bitter finish. I tell him so. A glint in his eyes, and that mischievous grin: "Hee, hee!" Ayahuasca is notoriously foul-tasting, so I interpret his giggle as a 'you just wait and see' aside. I'm then offered a sip of lukewarm bitter coffee as a chaser. It goes down less well. As with all the others in the group, Scott embraces me as one would a loved one setting out on a journey. "Have a good experience, brother."

Rachel is the last to drink, a tiny amount, barely a sip. She embraces Scott and he affectionately rubs her back. He then saunters over to the candle flame in the centre of the circle and extinguishes it with a swipe of a bamboo fan. It's a dramatic flourish that plunges the spaceship into darkness. I lie on my mat, not sure what to do. Should I try to meditate? I remind myself that I'm standing at the gateway to the unknown, that I should be relishing the crackle of anticipation. A barrage of thoughts comes, distracting me from the here-ness of the moment, the expectant energy, the rain falling over the psychotropic forest. And then, a voice cuts through my thought stream, at once both plaintive and vigorous, the sound of *icaros,* songs sung in ceremony by the shamans to invoke benevolent spirits. These will continue throughout the ceremonies, shared between Scott's two Peruvian assistants. I've read that *icaros* are beautiful and comforting and can ground you if you're feeling anxious or unsafe. I listen willingly, hopeful of tuning into this golden frequency but all I can muster is mild irritation. The shaman's voice is nasal and shrill, invasive. Later, the second shaman will showcase his particular brand – an impossibly deep-throated, otherworldly ululation. Disappointingly, I will warm to neither.

The minutes and the *icaros* float by and nothing happens. Everyone is lightly anointed with rose water as the shamans move about the room. Then Doug, a hyper-intense, snowboarding Canadian who had taken three cups of medicine (copious by average standards) begins to retch violently. After four or five successive spews nothing remains in his system to eject. Soon after I hear laughter bubble out of him and then the words "My past isn't relevant! It's been wiped out!" This is followed by a volley of "*ahs*", and mumbled phrases that suggest a procession of insights. A few other people seem to be readying themselves for *la purga* – buckets are constantly being repositioned and trails of flashlight weave their way towards the toilet area in the event of a more problematic evacuation.

It's not long before I too notice the stirrings of nausea. It builds until I'm sure I'm going to puke, but frustratingly it hovers on the brink and remains there. I also begin to feel that *coming up* sensation I associate with LSD and MDMA – a sense of spaciousness and expansion growing inside me. I become lighter, more fluid. That ambivalent feeling of losing control and letting go begins to pervade me: I want it but I fear it. If I do let go, what do I let go into?

And now, something completely unexpected, unfathomable but deeply, clearly known occurs: I hear the distinct, unmistakeable sound of drilling. To my right, just within eyeshot, a creature, part-alien, part-abstract entity is hovering. She is composed of pin-points of green neon and she is operating on me. I am her patient. I see her burrowing down into my DNA and cellular energy body, coolly reconfiguring my innards, identifying what needs to shift where in order for healing to commence. She is my surgeon and her name is Ayahuasca.

*

The mother of all plant medicines, also known as 'the vine of the dead' is actually a concoction of the vine *Banisteriopsis caapi* (the ayahuasca plant) and *Psychotria viridis*, a leafy plant containing the potent psychoactive dimethyltryptamine (DMT). DMT, which is also present in other natural hallucinogens, is responsible for visionary experience and access to the spirit realm, however, when ingested by humans, it is metabolised by the stomach enzyme monoamine oxidase (MAO) thereby rendering it inactive. Therefore, in order for the DMT to work, a chemical is required to inhibit the action of the MAO. The ayahuasca plant contains such a chemical, making it an effective MAO-inhibitor. Thus, the DMT is able to circulate through the bloodstream and into the brain. This feat of engineering, probably discovered thousands of years ago, is astonishing in itself, but when you consider that there are over 80,000 species of plant in the Amazon, the odds of someone hitting upon this exact combination of plants to unleash the psychoactive payoff seems miraculous. It's not known for sure how this was discovered, although folklore suggests that the plants themselves communicated this information to shamans and healers.

The ayahuasca brew (or tea) is made by boiling the two component plants together in a cauldron and allowing them to simmer over the course of half a day or so. What remains following this process is the sludgy, dark chocolate-coloured liquid that is imbibed in the ceremony. At Refugio there is a constant production line of ayahuasca – plants harvested, ingredients boiled and bottled. The whole process is performed out in the open, and Scott frequently leads cooking demonstrations in an area between the ceremonial hut and the main communal building. As he talks us through the preparations, an armed guard loitering nonchalantly to his side, sinewy Peruvian men beat, chop and strip the plants to a stringy pulp. I wonder how many of them drink the final product.

*

I'm waiting to speak with Scott, sitting in the derelict waiting room-cum-library beneath his bedroom. Pieter is up there now, asking for advice on tonight's ceremony. He had not experienced anything during the first one and is anxious he'll leave the Amazon with nothing to take away with him. We are both running on empty, having had perhaps a total of six hours sleep since we left London four days ago. Today we swung in hammocks, watched an ayahuasca cooking demonstration and dipped in and out of conversation with the other guests, too wired to sleep, too exhausted to fully engage. We are particularly fond of a Canadian couple, Kathy and Mark, who have visited Refugio many times and have returned now because Kathy is struggling to fall pregnant. Ayahuasca, known to cure myriad illnesses and conditions, could be the answer. They're about our age, with a kindred sensibility. They've worked with other shamans and they swear by Scott. Yes, he's unconventional. Yes, there are rumours. But they don't question his expertise or his integrity. Mark explains that there are 'jungle politics' at play and that the guns are necessary for self-protection and to project a don't-fuck-with-me attitude. Scott owns a lot of land and employs many locals, and this doesn't sit well with rival land owners. At night, don't be alarmed when volleys of gunshot ring out over the forest; it's Scott's reminder of who's in charge. And the rumours concerning his sexual impropriety are more than likely the machinations of jealous adversaries or delusional, damaged people. And then there's the whole other issue of evil spirits…

When I meet with Scott I'm not sure what I really want from the encounter. Perhaps I simply want reassurance. After the alien surgeon episode in the last ceremony, nothing more had happened and I was left high and dry, head spinning. Once again I slip into earnestness and passionately state that I'm willing to experience whatever it takes in order to heal. Heal from what? He doesn't ask, and in that moment I don't think I actually know. But there's an injury of some sort, otherwise I wouldn't be here. Right? I know this, at least I tell myself I do, but how do I know? Could it be that this need to heal simply fits into my abiding personal narrative, the one constructed by my ego? I have also long championed the notion that my injury explains my drive to be a therapist. I identify with the archetype of the *wounded healer*, and have spent years poring over the origins of the hurt only to arrive at a place in my life where I no longer feel compelled by my 'story' and have, at least consciously, given it up. But, then again, my giving up the story may just be another story. I ask Scott what led him to being a therapist and then a shaman. He explains, casually, how he one day dropped to his knees and asked God to give him the power to heal or he would stop pursuing this work. "And this was granted me." He goes on to tell me that my presence is in itself healing; he noticed my inner-serenity when we first met. What's more, ayahuasca is already working on me. After the next ceremony, I would find that my consciousness has expanded "25-30% upward", and that everything I do – films I see, music I listen to, encounters with others – will take on this new expanded perspective. "And then, in six months' time, you'll be back to continue the journey." I like the sound of this, but I wonder if it can be that simple. "Be careful not to get rid of the fighter part of you, brother. You'll need it", he says as I leave. As I walk back to our house in the dusky half-light, wearily traipsing through mud and swatting away insect-heavy air, I wonder what he means. I also wonder what the hell I'm doing and for a brief interlude, softened by all these questions, I fall into an inexplicable sadness.

*

There is no coming to consciousness without pain

C. G. Jung

The evening of the second ceremony. I go up for my cup of medicine and, feeling bullish, request a larger dose. Scott nods sagely, pours me a full cup. It tastes wretched: sour, bloody, utterly foreign. Then another three quarters of a cup, rounded off with a mouthful of coffee. A hug from Scott. I return to my mat and settle in for what's to come.

Twenty minutes of darkness and *icaros* pass. I veer off into distraction and vague mind chatter. Will I meet the alien again? Is Pieter okay? What if we're all deluded and chasing the tail of wish-fulfilment? Is this simply misplaced hedonism masquerading as spiritual quest? And then, weaving its way through the questions, burrowing to the surface from somewhere deep inside of me, the dawning of a sensation. It begins as gentle disorientation and then morphs into something altogether darker. I'm restless and uncomfortable without knowing why, so I try moving into a seated position in the hope that this will steady me. It doesn't. Perhaps if I puke? I fumble around for the bucket but I know I'm not ready to purge. Even so, I crouch over it, imitating the posture of someone about to spew his guts out. Breathing in the bucket's plastic emptiness, I begin to feel the stirrings of panic. A realisation descends: I'm in trouble.

How does a writer convey, in words, that which is beyond language? Or pre-language? Language-less. He will of course fail, but there's pathos in trying. It's perhaps his duty to try, in the hope that the ineffable can be communicated, trounced and tamed. I kindle that hope now, as I write this from a necessary distance, but in that moment of panic, peering into the bucket's unblinking nothingness, there is no hope. There is only dread. It's as if I've mainlined pure fear and my body is too slight to contain it. It swirls and expands through me, threatening to implode. My brain presses against my skull, my heart accelerates. I am pathetic with helplessness, unable to marshal any resources. *Please make this stop!* And yet I know that it won't. *Then let me die!* But death would be too easy, too kind. No, I will have to endure this. This...what? For a time – I have no idea how long – there is no answer, just the stark, stupefying horror of the Unknown. But whereas I had previously considered the Unknown to be, if not benevolent then at least neutral, it has now blindsided me by revealing itself to have a torturous nature. And then the answer comes tumbling forward like a comet, fully formed, previously known but forgotten: I have no doubt that I am in hell. It is circular, with spirals that descend to lower levels where the process of wretchedness is repeated. Each time I near the end of a process I prime myself to purge, nausea begging to be released. But nothing comes. I stick my fingers down my throat – dry gagging. Descending to the next layer, the horror of repetition. There is no way out. It is endless, timeless. Eternal damnation. I'm so utterly, exquisitely alone that I watch myself mouth the words, "Father, why hast thou forsaken me?" And in that moment, having never before paid him more than a cursory, quizzical thought, I know Jesus. The Crucifixion, the Holocaust, Pain: I know them. Is it possible that I have *asked* for this? It seems obscene. And yet here I am, deep in the Amazon, burning in hell, wishing I was dead. It's my only lifeline now, a miserable, puny succour: *I asked for this.*

The ordeal is multi-dimensional. It's as if several tracks are playing at once. So even though I'm consumed by inner trauma, I'm simultaneously aware of what's happening around me. Scott approaches, wearing a headlamp to navigate his way through the dark space. I feel his presence, and then his gentle touch. I try to communicate the extent of my distress but it's like trying to speak from beneath a roaring wave. He's mumbling, moving his hands over my body, blowing cool air over me. "I'm going to move the energy, turn down the intensity." I want to say thank you but I'm not sure the words come out. As he continues to work on me, fleeting, sickening thoughts tumble out: *He's made a mistake. I shouldn't be feeling like this. He gave me too much. I'm in serious trouble.*

All the while, another track is playing at a different frequency: my mind scrambling to make sense of this nightmare. The thoughts are scattershot at first, too weak to organise themselves against the tirade of raw pain, but gradually a sense begins to emerge, of a memory stored in my body, a trove of knowledge both accessible and deeply hidden all these years.

> *I am an infant, perhaps two years old. My body is racked with illness, it is bruising from the inside and there are purple blotches the size of plates all over me. It's a rare condition. I'm admitted to hospital, and because I protest so vehemently when my mother leaves, the doctors forbid her to visit me again. In response, I batter my head against the cot, inconsolable. My mother's sudden absence = the end of the world, total annihilation.*
>
> *This abandonment is itself a replaying of another, earlier trauma. My father had unconsciously declared war on me after my birth, experiencing me as a rival for my mother's attention. The physical bruising is a manifestation of his psychic attack, his unconscious wish*

to do me in. So the abandonment I experience is a double one. But what emerges now, in the midst of my isolation, is a vivid empathy for my father's own trauma: his mother, never fully available to him due to her own unresolved grief at losing her mother when she was a child, effectively abandoned him all his life. My mother rescued him from the ongoing abandonment. My birth made my father an orphan again.

These insights build and resonate until I realise that I am carrying not only my own pain, but the wounds of generations. My parents' pain. Their parents', and their parents' parents… I fall backwards through the ages, tumbling through the murk of accumulated hurt, and as I recede so the bile rises. I pull the bucket towards me and hang my head over it. A wave of hot, sour puke gushes out, so intense it feels as if it's leaking from my eyeballs. A short respite and then another spew. And another. By the fifth round there is nothing more to expel except for the dry echo of what's come before. I spit out the curdled breath, wipe away tears and mucous. I sense the worst is over but I'm not out of the woods yet. Curling into a crumpled ball, I wait to emerge from intensive care.

*

In real time, a ceremony lasts between three and five hours. But by the end, when Scott and the participants are mingling and sharing experiences in the sober candlelight, the concept of time has been rendered, if not meaningless, then at least suspect. How do you measure the amount of time it takes to relive the primal past? Does one hour in eternity feel shorter than two? Although I'm back in clock time, aware of it being around midnight, I still feel incubated and compromised, unable to walk for more than a few steps or to socialise in even the most basic way. I attempt to move towards Pieter, a few mats away from me, anxious to find out if he's okay. On my way there, Rachel appears, so radiant and sharply defined to my sensitive eyes that I can't look directly at her. She wants to know how I am, if I need any assistance. I watch myself mouth words, but there's no sound. Still, she seems to hear me, and the next thing I know we are engaged in a conversation I can't follow. All I'm aware of is the magnitude of her face. It appears moon-like, with crags of sadness etched into her skin. She is smiling, voice almost lilting, and yet all I hear is a hollow drone. Somehow I manage to survive this encounter and make my way to Pieter. I sit by his side and hold him as he lies in a heap, whimpering and juddering like a sick animal. It's distressing to witness but also a relief to shift my attention from a preoccupation with my own pain to attempting to console his. Having to step up into the role of carer enables a sense of dignity to return, and although I'm still frayed and fragile, I now have a purpose I can cling to. The stark and abiding fact of our love is luminous amongst these psychic ruins.

Gradually everyone leaves the spaceship, leaving the two of us in darkness. We will remain here for the rest of the night, watched over by a guard, too overwhelmed to find our way back to our house. Everyone appears to have had an easy (or easier) ride, some even sound euphoric. Father, why hast thou forsaken us?

*

I walk through the next day with my head in a cloud of self-pity and wonder. Nothing looks the same. The grass, mud, tea, clouds: they appear reassuringly themselves whilst bearing an invisible current of portent, as if they are metaphors for something else, something belonging to a grand, sinister design. Incredulous at what I was put through and petrified that it might happen again in the evening's ceremony, I return to the spaceship in the late afternoon, kneel down and pray for mercy. It's the first time I've ever prayed, and even though I'm not sure who or what exactly I'm praying to, the act of doing so feels obligatory. At this moment in time I am humbled to a degree I never before thought possible. And a realisation is dawning: that, contrary to my self-perception as a deeply empathic therapist, what I have discovered is that I have never truly known suffering and therefore have never been fully present to the pain of others. Is this what ayahuasca has been waiting to show me? Yes, it is, I decide. The jungle has summoned me for this very reason. I asked for it. But when I mouthed the words, two days ago, "I want to work more deeply with my clients", I knew not what I was asking for. If I had known what the prescription would turn out to be, I would not have asked for it.

Perhaps even more startling than this revelation is the realisation that suicide had appeared so desirable. I think I understand now, for the first time, what might drive such a choice. Wading through the quagmire of hell, with no end in sight, death appears the only relief. Even with an end in sight (in the thick of the trip I was aware that the effects were time-limited) death still spoke convincingly to me. Had I been on my own, with only Scott's gun for company, who knows what might have transpired? My personal threshold for pain is either way lower than I had ever imagined, or simply meaningless in the face of pure suffering. In the aftermath of last night's awakening, life trembles with fresh, wet vulnerability. I traverse Refugio Altiplano looking for Scott, hoping he can dispense reassurance, an explanation or at least confirm my fears that I have unluckily stumbled into a black hole of trauma, but he's nowhere to be found. My abandonment feels complete.

Somehow, despite the fear, I find myself back for another ceremony that evening, gingerly downing half a cup of ayahuasca and continuing to pray to Whatever. The smaller dose, coupled with my reluctance to let go, sets the tone for a largely eventless ceremony. There's a moment of panic near the beginning when I experience foreboding sensations of ebbing away into a black space flecked with green microdots. I tense against the pull and try to remain on the surface of the dread rather than getting sucked under. It's a bit like the sensation I had as a child, screwing up my eyes against the dark and falling back into space. After this initial worry, the sense of danger recedes and I begin to tap into a layer of spaciousness and calm, an intuition that I will be held and protected. Insights come, but they are intellectual rather than embodied: *I need to let go so that I can let love in. The spaciousness I feel is not separate from me – it* is *me. Trust what emerges.*

The next day there is no ceremony. A few of us take a boat ride to a neighbouring village, Magdalena, population 80. We visit a ramshackle school, deserted until late afternoon because of the heat. In the cool of a makeshift convenience store we sip juice from freshly felled coconuts and chew cheap sweets. Mangy cats, monkeys and iguanas quietly bake in the sun. Later in the day we sweat out toxins in a custom-built sauna near the river's edge. Throughout the day Everything But The Girl's 'Walking Wounded' is on repeat in my head, a comforting reminder that trauma can be transformed into art and made palatable. You can even hum along to it.

That night, as the jungle is pelted by another ferocious storm, we fall into our first proper sleep since leaving London. I dream I'm lying in my father's childhood bed, feeling afraid. I get up and notice, on the threshold between the bedroom and the corridor, two large (possibly dead) rats and a shiny black dog. What happens next is a muddle. I then dream of my childhood home. It's being redecorated, stripped of all its furniture and transformed into a vast white cube.

*

It's the evening of the final ceremony. I'm meditating in the hammock on our porch, absorbing the fading light and the incessant chatter of birds and insects. Pieter is painting – the first time he's done so in years. Whereas I need to write or talk things through in order to process them, he makes sense of his experience by silently digesting it, perhaps translating it into images and abstract impressions until it distils into intuition. He's been bruised by ayahuasca too, having lived through a kind of rebirthing, his body still shuddering involuntarily with stabs of electric energy. It's like that scene in the Road Runner cartoon where Wile E. Coyote electrocutes himself and for days after is still randomly buzzing like a live wire. Fast forward a few months, and we are lying in bed holding one another, and I feel his body jolt against mine, an echo of this short-circuiting anomaly.

Before the ceremony, I meet with Scott for a final time. I pass the armed guard who announces my arrival by shouting up into the trees. Scott gives the okay for me to ascend. As I climb the wooden staircase towards the third floor landing, I once again notice the complete lack of anything vaguely domesticated about this living space. It resembles a building site in suspended process, planks of wood strewn about, a pair of gumboots stranded here, a whiskey bottle harbouring spiders there. On the level just below the bedroom there are shelves of dusty books – novels, anthropology, mysticism – a gesture towards a library. And littered throughout the room, in nestling clumps, bottles of various shapes and sizes containing the mother lode, the iron-blood-bilious-brew, ayahuasca. There's enough here to fuel thousands of ceremonies. Revolutions, even. What if all world leaders were obliged to drink this portal-opening, ego-obliterating cocktail? Imagine – politics informed by plant wisdom; humility and vulnerability valued over greed and guile. But I'm running ahead of myself. I'm here for some last minute reassurance, a fatherly hug. I want my revolution to be bloodless.

"Brother, how are you? Good to see you." Scott's on the bed, next to Rachel, sifting through what look like official documents. He's wearing nothing but a towel around his waist. Fleetingly, I glimpse his penis as he shifts position. I wonder if the two of them have just had sex. Rachel politely leaves the room, trailing a scent of melancholy in her wake. I still can't decide whether she's robust or brittle, or both. She seems to have completely subjugated herself to the jungle, to Scott: an act of either supreme courage or fear.

Scott seems agitated. "Got half way to Iquitos on the motorboat yesterday and it happened. Motor caved in. So, what to do? We wait. Nobody's getting anywhere. Finally dived in and swam the rest of the way. Some days that kinda thing's just gonna happen!" He continues to rummage through his documents, one of which looks like a passport. He's planning a trip to the US, he tells me. Meeting with investors. He has big plans for Refugio Altiplano. I can see he's busy and I don't want to keep him, so I launch into it. *Any advice for the last ceremony? I don't want to leave with nothing but trauma to show for my efforts.* I'm once again plunged into that adolescent feeling that is both unnerving and soothing: I surrender myself to Father, to the Unknown. Scott stops what he's doing and gives me his full attention. He seems to recognise my anxiety. As he talks, he appears to be conjuring words from the ether, or from the subconscious. Sentences begin in a muddle, sounds oozing out of a vortex but swiftly crystallised into straightforward, no-nonsense offerings: "Your energy is more balanced now. The toxins have been cleared out. You're younger now than you were when you arrived...Focus on your third eye in the ceremony; this is the plane of higher consciousness and ayahuasca elucidates it...If the devil shows up tonight, you gotta shoo him away, show him who's boss. You say, *I've got no time for you*, and you – hee, hee! – swat him away like a fly. Simple as that."

He tells me he knows all about hell. During his shamanic training he spent two weeks on the knife's edge between sanity and madness. There was no saying which way he'd fall. My whole being recoils at the thought of spending so long in this state. I had been there for a few hours and it had been unbearable. But two weeks? I would have ended my life, no doubt about it. I'd always prided myself on being able to live in the unknown, to face mystery with equanimity, but Scott had blown my cover: my ability to live without knowing was nothing more than lip service, a thinly disguised defence against the real thing. I would certainly be returning to London, and to my psychotherapy practice, with my tail between my legs.

"What are the chances I'll go back to hell tonight?" I ask, facing the full force of my fragility. Scott's response is at first fluid and unequivocal: "No", he says, "you've done that now. That's all over." He says this as if he's addressing me out of character, as if these words are pure fact, unfiltered through the guise of personality. For a moment, there is no Scott, no shaman. But then, after a pause, he somehow re-emerges: "Then again, you never know."

*

The final ceremony. A few new seekers here tonight including Rob, a personal trainer from Boston whose raw food diet and weight-lifting regime have rendered him impossibly buff and chiselled; and Jennifer, a loud and confident Wall Street broker who's been visiting Refugio since it opened in the 90s. She has a gap in her busy schedule and has flown in for a 'top up'. If this makes ayahuasca seem like a botox injection administered on the hoof, it would belie the sense I have of a woman who, contrary to appearances, nurses a secret pang for self-realisation.

Fifteen minutes after drinking my half cup (as putrid-tasting as ever), the foreboding sense of trouble begins to creep up on me. It reaches a crescendo, threatening but not overwhelming. Patterns, lattice-like grids begin to flood my vision, twirling and twisting through hyperspace. I allow myself to get lost in the geometry but then the thought *What if this turns sinister?* appears, and on cue a spiky dragon-like shape looms in from the side, as if to test me. I easily shoo it away, just as Scott had advised. This boosts my confidence and I let go of a parcel of fear. My command feels effortless as I experiment with banishing other devils-in-disguise, and I discover that I'm able to navigate my mind with a certain dexterity. I can choose, for example, to follow linguistic lines of inquiry, delving into words and bringing out their essences and beating hearts, or I can select the visual realm and open to the wild ride of images – cupcakes, marionettes, serpents' tails, laser lights flying at me. But I realise that I'm not interested in these visions, if anything they only distract from what's brewing intuitively beneath the surface. And, just as Scott had described it, these insights can be plugged into by concentrating awareness on the energy of the third eye, in the space between my eyebrows:

> *I am the best of my mother (heart) and father (mind). An integration of mother and father balances the shamanic equation of male/female, which is the sweet spot, the source of wholeness. I have known this intellectually but now the knowing is felt and authentic. This authenticity allows me to help others in their own authentic uncovering.*
>
> *I realise that my days as a boy are over. I'm ready to be a man. I forgive my father his temporary abandonment of me. What's more, I am proud of him, and deeply appreciative that I've inherited some of his strengths.*
>
> *When it's appropriate, I too can be a father. To myself, to my clients, to my unborn child, should he or she ever materialise.*
>
> *This wisdom is always accessible, if I will just let go of fear. Letting go allows intuition to emerge, to take root.*
>
> *To let go is to be enlightened.*

The insights come effortlessly and steadily and bring with them a state of heightened wellbeing. Even so, I intuit that this is but a mere inkling of what is possible. I've expended so much energy on protecting myself that there's not been enough left over to seriously power the cruising altitude I'm now experiencing. Tomorrow we leave the jungle and head back to our routines. If I really want to know the true potential of ayahuasca, I will need to start planning my return to Refugio Altiplano.

*

A revolution takes time to settle in

Lanza del Vasto

Back in London the routine of daily life quickly moulds us back into shape. Nothing has changed on the surface, but we're both aware of a deep inner disruption spreading through our DNA like a fissure in the earth's crust. A process unleashed. I don't know what to do with it, but I try to embrace the unknowing. I sometimes catch myself shaking my head in disbelief at what happened, tears welling for reasons unclear. My attempts to explain my jungle experience to friends and family fall wildly short of doing it justice, and I begin to feel that talking about it degrades it. Perhaps silence is the noblest recourse.

After a couple of weeks, I drop Scott an email. We had not got to say a proper goodbye the morning we left Refugio (he was possibly busy fending off alligators during his morning river swim), so I send my deepest gratitude and thanks, and wonder if, in the hubbub of people coming and going through his psychotropic doors, he would even remember me. A few days later I receive his response:

> Hello Paul, Thank you for your attention and friendship. You and Pieter are good friends of mine and can always expect to be welcome here in my off-the-grid evolution reserve in the rainforest. Take good care of yourselves and remember that you have your ally here in the jungle.
>
> Abrazos, Scott.

I google the English translation of *abrazos*: hugs. I'm immediately back in his manly, compassionate embrace.

For the next few months I live consciously with my hard-won insights, attempting to integrate them through meditation, reading, writing and reflection. As a therapist, I feel different – more vulnerable, more tender, more able to connect with people's suffering, to be moved by it and to contain it. The texture of my presence is finer, calmer. The more I talk about the experience, the more it settles into the Known, into fact. When I travel home to South Africa for a brief visit I tell my parents about the ceremonies, sparing nothing, and it's a cathartic experience for us. I return to London and begin work on my Master's thesis which has been largely inspired by my time in the jungle. Through all this time Pieter and I are intent on planning our return visit and have many conversations about when next to go. We finally agree on dates and I write to Scott to request a booking but, uncharacteristically, he doesn't get back to me.

After a few days a friend of mine who is also considering a trip to Refugio, tells me that she's been to the website where there's a posting of upsetting news. Scott Petersen is dead. The truncated announcement reads: *We have lost a visionary and a great shaman. He had an accident and now he rest [sic] in peace with mother nature. And those who have had the fortune to meet him, we will keep your legacy in our hearts.*

I search the rest of the site but there is no further explanation. I google 'Scott Petersen death' and a ribbon of links cascades down the page. *Scott Peterson pictured on death row...a decade after he killed his wife.* It transpires that all of the links deal with this other Scott, so I re-google 'Scott Petersen Refugio Altiplano'. Along with his website, a few other entries appear, all familiar to me. Some of them are the rants of disgruntled bloggers claiming that Scott is a drunk and a sexual predator. One Facebook entry reads: *Scott Petersen [...] must have a reason for hiding in the jungles of Peru. He would all ready [sic] be in jail if he were behaving like this in other parts of the world!! [...] I am relieved to see that a woman had the courage to speak up about Scott Petersen's abusive actions at Refugio Altiplano. I too had a disturbing and frightening experience when I visited Refugio Altiplano last summer. I intended to stay ten days, but left much earlier because there were too many signs that indicated that the longer I remained there, the chances of him sexually violating me would increase.*

The blogger goes on to describe a series of encounters with Scott in which he tried to force himself on her. She also makes disturbing claims about his behaviour in general: *No one knew how Scott would react to them because he's drunk most of the time. He swore at people and treated them with no respect. He is a power hungry, ego maniac and operates Refugio Altiplano as a money making business. Healing is secondary and not a priority.*

Below this entry is a Facebook conversation in which readers have posted their responses. Some of them concur with this depiction of Scott, saying they too had experienced his lecherousness. Only one person expresses her disbelief, based on what she's experienced of him, which, she confesses, is limited to watching his online talks. But there are many positive, even effusive reports (many from women) on other sites such as TripAdvisor: *Scott is undoubtedly the finest Shaman we have had the privilege to witness. His passion for his life's work is apparent the moment you meet him and his knowledge of medicinal plants is second to none...* reads a typical, five star review. And there is a wealth of reviews that pay homage to the safe environment he has created and to his integrity.

And what of Rachel, I wonder. I can't imagine what she'll do now without Scott to shape and contain her lostness. Will she return to her previous existence in the States, or somehow soldier on down the shamanic path, wounded and resolute? I should email her, I decide; reach out to a fellow traveller, another broken soul. But something inside me knows I won't.

I keep checking the internet for news and a few days later I learn that Scott fell from his third floor balcony, and broke his neck. In the absence of any further elucidation, a number of possibilities present themselves: It was an accident. He'd been drinking and lost his step. Foul play suspected: jungle politics finally caught up with him (where was his gun, or his guards, when he needed them?) Evil spirits did him in. He consciously chose to end his life and transition to the next plane. Each explanation seems absolutely plausible to me. And even though I'm shocked at the suddenness of the death of a man who I had experienced as so gregariously vital, so luminous in his masculinity yet deeply respectful of his feminine aspect, even so I find myself profoundly unsurprised by the shape and form of his death which, for a man who lived on the edge, seems to me to be entirely harmonious and in keeping with the life that came before it.

*

Post-script: 15 months after ayahuasca.

Is it glib to say that everything's different and yet it's the same? After all, everything changes all the time, from moment to moment, even if on the surface appearances seem unaltered.

I would like to believe that a profound transformation has occurred as a result of my jungle experience. I have my journal, my memories, the lingering felt sense of annihilation and expansion. I'm more patient with pain, more compassionate. Ego is still very much alive, of course, and if I'm not paying attention it can sneakily pass itself off as humility when in fact what it's really after is admiration: *You did that? You went to hell all in the name of self-growth? Impressive!*

I would also like to believe that, while in the transitional space of the Amazon, I met my transitional father, who, with assistance of the Plant Mother, helped me over a personal psychic threshold and into real adulthood. It all makes perfect psychological sense. On some level, I know it to be true.

But could it also be that I have fashioned, from trauma, a narrative that must, at all costs, make sense of what would otherwise be too horrendous to contemplate: putting my trust in the hands of a wayward gringo, having him play recklessly with my soul, and then playing too recklessly with his own? In my need for a father, did I see in him love and wisdom rather than charisma, opportunism and indifference? Is it possible that he is all these things, light and dark, as am I? The more I inquire into ayahuasca, Scott, and me, the less I seem to know.

The questioning stirs me into retracing the path from my early, heady London days to where I now find myself. I've sporadically written diaries over the years, many of which I've thrown away, but there are a few that remain, unread since I wrote them, tucked away on the bottom shelf of a bookcase. I find one dating back to the summer of 1999, our second year in London. It details my training with Daniel, including accounts of my dreaming sessions in which I encounter my animal guide (a camel), merge with trees, travel to 'the orange planet' and learn to tap into the dynamic force field of universal energy. I write about needing to understand suffering, about moving my 'assemblage point' from my head to my body, learning to be humble and patient. "I am drowning in my own unease…fear, fear, fear. I have to face it alone." It feels so familiar and yet so far away. The words wash over me after a few pages, a wave of self-pity and purple prose spelling out my rudderless life. But in the midst of it, in an entry ruminating over a period of sexual frustration and experimentation, a phrase hurtles forward, as sharp and chilling as a shark's fin: "Twice rejected by a *Scott*. What's in that name?"

After that first ceremony, the one in which the green alien announces her arrival with drill and intent, I am dazed and speculative, trying to enter into conversation with fellow participants but fumbling for words and semblance. Drunk but sharp. Pieter is by my side, also at a loss. Scott ambles up to us and offers hugs. He asks how we're doing.

After that, my memory is hazy. I think Pieter asks a question, and Scott, in characteristic fashion, begins mumbling a response. His weathered voice ebbs and flows and at some point I give up trying to follow his thread. But then he says something that leaps out at me, sobers me up. It emerges from a muddle until I clearly hear him say: "You gotta let the unconscious come out, you know, just let it do its thing, and then it speaks to you, you know, it's crazy stuff, Bugs Bunny and Elmer Fudd..."

I laugh, partly out of surprise and partly out of the joy of recognition, because I have written a novel, *Rabbit Season*, which takes its title from a Bugs Bunny cartoon. It's about a boy who attempts to deal with childhood trauma (being abandoned by his parents) by escaping into a cartoon reality. Scott, who does not know about my Bugs Bunny connection, notices my reaction, turns to me and, as if directly addressing my unconscious, says, "Hee-hee! You know exactly what I'm talking about, brother, don't you?"

Yes, Scott. I think I do.

The Art of Not-Knowing: From Archetypal Encounter to Psychological Integration

Jason P. Ranek

This is a story about living in relation to mystery. It is a true story, though parts of it might seem fantastic to some. I myself have at times fallen into doubt over it, as some of it is very far removed from everyday life experience. But the memory is indelible, and I can only conclude that it actually happened, however strange it still seems. To say it happened, however, does not assume knowledge of *what* actually happened; that the experience might have been a mental aberration is not out of the question. In fact, the question of definitions is at the heart of what this story is about. The unknown, the mystery, is all around us at all times – usually disguised as the known, the understood, the thoroughly comprehended. Still, every so often, the veil is ripped asunder and we come face to face with phenomena that defy explanation and leave us at the mercy of our partial and imperfect knowledge. If in that moment we are honest and do not resist the vertigo of not-knowing, then a great gift is given to us: the gift of awe. This is the beginning of the spiritual life.

My life has been ordinary for the most part. But that is to say that, like most lives, it has been littered with the fantastic and weird. Yet because those times do not easily align with the rest of our lived experience, they can easily get shelved away and almost forgotten, as this story nearly was. Thus, one of the keys to cultivating a spiritual life is attention.

Almost two years ago, in the midst of gripping depression and marital problems, I travelled to Amsterdam to participate in a Brazilian religious ceremony that involved the drinking of a powerful psycho-active brew concocted from rain forest plants. My hope was that the ensuing visions would offer healing, and a new direction for my troubled life. The visions never came. The fact is, I had already received my vision some four years previous, but because I had not paid sufficient attention, I had forgotten, and had not yet begun to claim the riches of the experience.

But it was not just lack of attention; the truth is I never fully came to terms with the mysterious nature of the incident. With unconscious arrogance, I had proceeded to dissect, categorise and explain the unknown and unknowable. I took what was a gift of immense power – powerful enough to fuel a sense of awe over an entire lifetime – and turned it into an object amenable to rational analysis. I actually know precious little about what happened to me that January day; I do know, however, that presuming knowledge where I had none, and assuming familiarity where there wasn't any, robbed the experience of its transformative power. No doubt the reader is now impatient to get to the story. But let me preface it with a brief autobiography so that the context is roughly sketched.

I was born in the mid-western United States to a devout Catholic family, the youngest of five children. Religion played a central role in the lives of my parents, and I was immersed in the ceremonies and rituals of the Church from an early age. I remember attending early morning daily Mass with my mother before I was old enough to go to school. Because my family had suffered the tragic loss of my mother's sister and her family two years before I was born, one of the earliest life lessons I unconsciously imbibed was that religion is a refuge from the trials of this world.

My adolescence was marked by a period of rebellion, coupled with an intense interest in my Catholic heritage, the bible and world religions in general. I remember buying a hardcover copy of John B. Noss's *Man's Religions* at a rummage sale for twenty-five cents, and poring over it lovingly for hours on end. The summer when I was fifteen, my parents took me to the Smithsonian in Washington D.C. With some time to kill on my own, I wandered – by accident – into the Freer Art Museum, which houses one of the world's premier collections of Asian art. There I encountered fantastic images of Buddhas and Bodhisattvas in painting and sculpture. I was transfixed for hours, lingering over these images of saints and sages from the East. It was a pivotal and formative experience. When a voice on a loudspeaker announced that the museum would be closing in fifteen minutes, I ran downstairs to the gift shop and spent all the money I had on books about Buddhism.

But a long shadow had been cast across my life. Beginning as a teenager, I began to suffer from protracted periods of depression, a condition which continued into adulthood and eventually came to be characterised by acute anxiety. I was also prone to acting out emotionally, and at times unpredictably. My life was chronically disrupted by this condition, and the energy I expended just to get by was wildly disproportionate to the everyday challenges I faced. Many were the remedies I ventured to try: psychotherapy, medication, hospitalisation, charismatic prayer, religious pilgrimage (accompanied by a strong faith in miracles), Native American healing ceremonies, and later, vast amounts of alcohol. (That last item should illustrate how many of my difficulties as a young adult were self-inflicted.) I suffered and learned a great deal, but I was still immature enough to believe in a magic bullet cure. Doing the heavy lifting of cultivating attention and self-awareness were lessons I had been exposed to in my study of Buddhism, but I couldn't be bothered; I was busy chasing the white rabbits of pain relief and pleasure, or looking for a final, comprehensive cure. In spite of the bumpy ride, I graduated college, more or less in one piece, with a degree in Fine Arts and – God help me – ambitions to be a poet.

Fast forward eleven years: I was married with three children, had published a small collection of poetry, and was living in Norway, my wife's country of origin. My infatuation with alcohol had been set aside, and my interest in Buddhism had at last blossomed into a commitment of sorts, and a daily practice. I had also found gainful employment as a delivery driver – not a job I had ever envisioned for myself, but one that paid the bills in a country where my particular CV was thoroughly unmarketable. But in spite of the relative stability of my life, I was chronically dysthymic, unhappy with my career prospects, and struggling to nurture my relationships in the face of my own sense of failure. I took some solace in religious practice, but was still in the difficult early years when the teaching has yet to penetrate the heart and self-discipline is a constant trial. My life worked, but just barely.

A well-worn chestnut of spiritual wisdom states, "When the student is ready, the teacher appears". However ill-prepared I might have been, it was time for me to meet one of my teachers.

I was delivering FedEx on one of the large islands jostling the coastline south of my wife's hometown. It was early January. The roads were caked with fresh snow, and the sun was low despite it being early afternoon. I had lived here long enough to understand that winter in modern Norway is still a time of leanness; for those of us who grew up in climes further south, the brevity of daylight is a lack one never fully comes to terms with. But for what one loses in sheer luminosity and vitamin D, there is payback of sorts: on clear days, the quality of light is exquisite. Everything takes on a numinous, timeless aspect, painted with a wide palette of golden hues and luxurious shadows. Overcast days are pure Norwegian granite (both in colour and melancholic density), but cloudless days are the antique brass of early morning all day long. Such was the light on that particular January afternoon.

String Valley Road winds lazily through farms and stretches of woodland, passes a small lake and finally descends to a rocky coast dotted with boat docks. Oblivious to the scenery, I turned up the heat in the cabin of my old Toyota van and considered how best to negotiate the driveway of the house where I was to deliver a pallet of textile packages from China. I felt like Amundsen on his way to the Pole, strategising how best to manoeuvre his train of men and materiel across an ice field pocked with crevasses. The driveway began as an incline that was long if gentle enough, but then turned left and descended sharply to a parking area beside a double garage. I knew from painful experience that, should I manage to make it up then down to the house, I would never get out – not with my rear-wheel drive, twelve-year-old veteran of a delivery van on a slope of new-fallen snow. I would be stuck until the road assistance truck arrived, or until some farmer came to pull me out with his tractor.

No, driving in was definitely not an option. But neither did the prospect of hoofing a whole pallet of packages up to the house from the main road hold any greater promise. Unloading would take nearly an hour, and the rest of my route would degrade into a fiasco of missed pickups and late deliveries. Truly, I was damned if I did or if I didn't, as I would bleed precious time in either case.

He came out of nowhere, a man of about seventy with flowing grey hair and a long, tangled beard. He stood at my van window and signalled me to roll it down. Even more arresting than his sudden, almost magical appearance, were his clothes: he wore a long robe of deep blue felted wool, boots of the same, and mittens of some sort of animal skin. The outfit gave an impression of native Sami or Siberian dress, though the man himself looked very Norwegian. He was slight of build, but the way he held his body spoke of a much younger man's strength. It took me a moment to take him in; he must have been walking quickly from somewhere, for he was breathing with gusto and exhaled thick clouds into the cold which caught the light and prevented me from seeing his face clearly. A second passed. Then the mist parted and I got a good look at him: the glacial-blue ice of piercing yet kindly eyes, the frozen moustache, the wind-raw cheeks and nose. Around his bare head, he wore what looked like a headband fashioned from a piece of white plastic. On it were inscribed letters, or perhaps symbols, written in what looked like ballpoint pen. I let my gaze linger there for a second, but the characters were unrecognisable, resembling what you might expect to see if someone tried to invent a space-alien alphabet. Taken in total, his appearance was more than vaguely shamanistic. Ever so slightly apprehensive, I rolled the window down.

"Can I help you?" he asked.

"Do you live in number thirty-five? I've got a whole pallet of packages for you if you do." His face registered nothing for a moment, but then lit up with a retrieved memory.

"Oh yes, those will be for my son. He's not home now, but you can drive up to the house and I'll help you unload."

I tensed. It was exactly what I didn't want to hear. Though the clock on the console of my van was digital, I could almost hear the seconds ticking away as I beheld what was certain to be an epic, time-wasting ordeal. But before I could respond, he began to march up the driveway, motioning with his mittened hand for me to drive after him. It wasn't a suggestion; he was *directing* me to follow. Given a pair of hypothetical evils, he seemed determined to ruin my day with the greater of the two.

Balking, I stuck my head out the window and tried to diplomatically point out what I thought to be obvious: "I don't think I'm going to make it out of your driveway if I go in there".

He spun around on his heel and looked at me directly with a lucid smile. "Don't worry! I'll help you. If you get stuck, I'll help you! I have a tractor parked up the road and I'll haul you out if I have to!" He spoke with an intensity that managed to catch me off guard. That he had a tractor stashed away somewhere struck me as dubious, given his obvious eccentricity; but I was short of options, so I rolled up the window and began to drive after him. The man's confidence was, if not contagious, at least persuasive.

"This is crazy", I said to myself.

I made it down to the garage without incident, and he began to help me unload the pallet, box by box, from the back of the van. Detecting my American accent, he switched to English and began to tell me about his visits to the US with the Norwegian Merchant Navy. He spoke energetically as we worked, and asked me all the usual questions – how long had I lived in Norway; how did I like it; did I miss home, etc. – and the interest he showed in my answers didn't seem the least bit feigned. Despite his age and the weight of the parcels, his pace was unflagging as he matched me box for box. Soon, his cheeks were flaring a darker shade of red, and the dripping faucet of his nose had grown a tiny icicle. With his long hair all crazy in the light, he chatted away until the last box was stowed safely away in the garage. The man was utterly unselfconscious, and almost pathologically friendly.

Finally, I collected his signature and began to consider the steep, snow-packed driveway before me. “Don’t worry, my friend; you’ll get out”, he said, patting me on the shoulder. Firing up the Toyota, I began to gently finesse the gas pedal as snow crunched beneath the slowly turning tires.

“I’ll push!” he yelled, and moved to the back of the van. Remarkably, I began to move. Inch by inch I crawled up the driveway, careful not to apply too much pressure to the gas, lest the van lose its purchase and the tyres spin. Ten feet. Twenty. But then he wasn’t pushing any more and had walked on ahead and was waving me up the slope with both arms as if I were steering a fighter jet ready for take-off and not a grunting package van. Unbelievably, I made it to the top of the driveway.

I stuck my head out the window. “I *cannot* believe it! Thank you, thank you for everything. I really appreciate the help...”

“You’re not out yet”, he said, and proceeded to walk me down the entire length of the driveway. At last, certain that I had reached the safety of the main road, he smiled and waved, then turned back toward the house now swaddled in shadow as the sun ran aground atop a distant ridge. From start to finish, the whole delivery had taken a mere twenty minutes.

I drove on, elated at my luck, and started to plan my next few stops. But I found it difficult to focus; the sun was setting, and the light had turned the stubble protruding through the snow-crusted fields to a luminescent violet. Something kept pulling me back to his face: that old, arresting, timeless face. What had happened back there? Why all the care and concern? It was as if he had made my anxieties his own, and then proceeded to obliterate them so as to reveal their insubstantiality. And why the headband? That silly piece of plastic with the hieroglyphs…

What happened next is difficult to explain. Here, my story enters a metaphysical field of experience that is radically subjective. I am uncomfortable with the term ‘mystical’ – an imprecise and much-abused word – as it by implication makes me a mystic. Truthfully, I can’t say for certain that the experience wasn’t self-generated. Whatever the case, the following events did not originate in my conscious mind; it was definitely not a daydream, and the feeling I had was one of being a passive recipient. But neither was I wholly unconscious of my physical surroundings. I was driving while it happened, and the elapsed time and distance, while fuzzy, are not beyond recall. From my perspective, it seemed that I was suddenly living in two worlds at the same time.

As I was driving northwest on String Valley Road, I suddenly found myself in a featureless, undefined space. The ambient emptiness was black. My body was 'there', for I was facing the man whom I had just left on the snowy drive a few minutes before, and there was a simple wooden chair standing between us. I remember feeling awkward at being there, as I intuited that he knew more about what was happening than I did. I also felt nervous, like at a visit to the doctor for an uncomfortable procedure. He gave me a squinty-eyed smile that turned the skin at his temples to a gaggle of crows' feet, and then spoke.

"I can help you." I couldn't help but notice an almost mischievous twinkle in his eye, as if he were about to do something that he shouldn't.

I tried to smile with what probably resembled a grimace. "How can you help me", I said. It wasn't a question but a statement. The tension in my mind was exquisite.

"Sit down." He motioned to the chair.

Inwardly I resisted, but just as I had followed him up the snowy drive, I sat down without protest. As I did, my perspective shifted as it sometimes will in a dream; I stood outside my body and saw myself sitting in the chair with him standing behind me. He closed his eyes and placed both his hands on my head.

"What are you—?"

"Shhhhhh," he whispered.

He seemed to be concentrating hard. I can remember feeling his hands on my head, but for me nothing else seemed to be happening. Not so for him; suddenly his face began to knot and twist, and every so often one of his shoulders would jerk as if some kind of energy were flowing through him and triggering his reflexes. After maybe forty-five seconds of this, the process seemed to intensify and to be causing him pain. Deep furrows appeared in his brow, and his breathing grew fast and irregular. Every so often it seemed as if he were about to say something, but the words never finished or rose above a whisper. I remember a twinge of shame that I should be feeling nothing but embarrassment as he suffered through some kind of ordeal – apparently on my behalf – but I was so overwhelmed with the strangeness of the affair that I couldn't have mustered a socially appropriate response to anything. Here, all my thoughts, words and actions were naked, unfiltered, real.

My self-consciousness vanished as he burst out with a loud shout. Then it became more than shouting; he was cursing and swearing. Suddenly, every kind of vulgar or obscene epithet imaginable was exploding from his mouth in a shockwave of white-hot rage. Spittle flew from his lips, though it seemed that sparks too were leaping from his body. It was surreal, for the kind old man I had met in the snow seemed incapable of radiating such blind, unchannelled fury. But that's precisely what it was: a kind of searing radiation. If gamma rays could be represented as language, they would sound as violent and corrosive. The energy coursing through his hands, still placed firmly on my head, was now palpable, but I barely noticed; and if in this place my body had any blood capable of running cold, it did. For in a flash I realised that the voice issuing from the old man's mouth – the voice cursing life and death, the disappointments of love, the loneliness of subjectivity; that hate-filled voice raging at the very fact of existence – was literally my own. All the pain and sadness, loathing and fear I had ever felt for myself or the world was manifesting through this timeless little man, and for the first time I heard what I sound like when caught in the throes of my anger.

Suddenly, he tore his hands from my head as if he had touched a hot stove and stumbled backward a couple steps. Arching his back, his chest expanded as if he were inhaling air enough for a multitude. I leapt up from the chair (my perspective had shifted back into my body) and turned around just in time to see a vast plume – no, a *fountain* of gold dust spray from his mouth, straight up into the air. There was a sound of wind as the geyser of pollen-like flecks of gold mushroomed and swirled through the blackness around us. It was dazzling: a self-illuminated cloud of gold, shimmering in the void. The jet lasted only a few seconds. He straightened himself, breathed deeply, then looked at me and smiled – obviously relieved of the pain – as the dust showered down everywhere, flaking his eyebrows and hair with brilliance. Soon, we were both glittering from head to toe.

I was breathless. "What did you do?!"

He smiled again and held up an open palm to let some of the sparkle alight there. Then shutting his eyes and turning his face up to bask in the blizzard of gold, he said, "I took the wounded, angry, fearful you and returned him to his original nature".

He said it matter-of-factly, as if it were all in a day's work, nothing special. But I felt strange, light – happy like I hadn't been in years. To say the weight had been lifted from my shoulders doesn't come close to capturing the feeling. It was as if the blinders had come off for the very first time. I was seized with a profound gratitude for my life, and as I mentally surveyed the landscape of my fears from this clear summit, I couldn't recognise a single problem. Everything was workable. Fear was insubstantial. Difficulties were actually grace. The world was still the world, but I saw it shining with a new light. Whoever and whatever this old man was, he lived in this light. He knew it, intimately. As the scene faded from my vision, I could still see his face, with that knowing, mischievous smile, luxuriating in the snowing radiance of original nature.

The remainder of the day passed in a daze of joy, with me effortlessly radiating friendliness to everyone I met. Even the guy at the auto repair place, who with an air of irritation signs for packages without a word, much less eye contact, was transfigured by the goodwill that had overtaken me. I couldn't help but smile and thank him as he abruptly turned back to his work, rolling up a sleeve with a greasy hand. Deep within, I was riding on repeating waves of energy and zest for the adventure that is life. The world seemed newborn, and everything was a discovery ready to unfold itself for my witness and reverence. I felt as if I had become Bodhisattva Never-Despising of the Lotus Sutra; I was internally bowing to everyone and everything I met, as all things were expressions of the living consciousness that is *being* itself – each an unfathomable mystery; each worthy of veneration. I felt like I had become a new man.

By that evening I was ecstatic. Returning home from work, I was determined to make contact with the old man again. Five minutes online yielded the phone number to his house. Having no idea what I would say, but not caring, I dialled. His son picked up. I gave a fumbling explanation about how I was the FedEx driver who had delivered the packages that day, and that his father had been an indispensable help and I had wanted to call and thank him personally.

"My father? Oh, yes. Well, he is a special case..." I was certain I could hear embarrassment in the silent registers of his voice.

"Well, he really was incredibly helpful, and I was wondering if I could just speak to him for a minute to thank him."

"I'm sorry", he said with mock regret, "but my father's turned in for the evening. He's old, you know; likes to get his sleep. I'll let him know you called."

No pass from the gatekeeper. I hung up, disappointed, but still feeling every corner of my mind suffused with a light not unlike the soft glow of the midwinter sun.

*

Despite initial appearances and my fervent hopes, this was not the magic bullet cure I had always been looking for. Within a few days I was back to feeling anxious and morose, and, much to my disappointment, still prone to being blown off course by the storms of life. But my encounter with the

Old Man archetype (I had immediately begun to read Jung) had been decisive; he'd held a mirror up to my essence – that is, the essence shared by all sentient beings – and I was able to see for the first time that it was gold. A subtle change had been initiated in my psyche, though it would take some years for me to see and appreciate the trajectory on which my life had been set. In the short term, things began to happen. Certain books began to fall into my hands. I started meeting people who were able to illuminate the path for me, especially the darker portions. My Buddhist practice intensified. Day by day, I was accumulating knowledge and experience which were moving me inexorably toward healing and greater wholeness of spirit.

But something else was happening as well. The more I read, the more convinced I became that I had plausible hypotheses to account for what had happened. Lest the reader think that I was after strictly conventional answers, I'll confess to entertaining quite supernatural scenarios alongside the rational ones. Eventually, though, I settled on a theory that answered the event to my satisfaction, and something amazing happened: I began to forget.

Not that this is entirely unnatural; no matter how intense or unique an experience, the sharpness of the memory will inevitably dull with time. But that is not the kind of forgetting I'm talking about. Because I believed my own explanation of the episode, I no longer needed it. Once something is comprehended, even wrongly, it necessarily sheds whatever mystery it once carried. It also loses the ability to excite wonder and nourish the imagination; and once the emotional healing I had experienced began to fade, what other purpose did the encounter with the Old Man serve if not to excite wonder and nourish my imagination? So along with the usual dimming of memory, I began to lose a sense of awe. For the presumption of knowledge, often called 'belief,' displaces wonder.

I wanted fiercely to meet him again. (Was this because I wanted to experience something else to rekindle the awe I was busy smothering with intellection?) I wanted to pin him down, if I could, and learn what was or wasn't true about this strange Old Man. Yet my conversation with the son had aroused my timidity; I was sure that repeated attempts at making contact would be unwelcome. So I waited. I actively sought delivery routes that would take me to String Valley Road in the hopes of meeting him outdoors, but he never appeared. I continued to read – especially in the Jungian tradition – and to refine my theory of what had happened. Time passed. And so did a sense of awe pass completely from my heart and mind. The memory had been dissected, analysed, and filed away for safe keeping, and was seldom taken out and savoured. But even then, the savouring was of a poor simulacrum, devoid of the hidden dimensions and pocket universes waiting in the memory unshackled from the presumption of knowledge.

Then one day I saw him. It was about a year later, again in the dead of winter. I was driving on the island in a rush to get to my next stop, and suddenly there he was. It happened so quickly that I barely had time to recognise him, let alone to consider putting a full stop to my route and talking with him. Besides, he looked busy. He was out in the middle of the field adjacent to his house digging what looked like a small grave, not unlike the ones I used to dig for baby caskets or crematory urns at the cemetery where I worked summers as a teenager. He was wearing the same outfit as before, and I could just make out the band of white plastic around his head. He was working slowly, obviously tired from his exertions, and the snow-dusted pile of dirt beside the hole was considerable. Clearly, whatever was going in was going in deep. (For some reason, I felt certain that something was going *in*, not coming out.) I smiled as I drove on: another mystery. There was no telling what he was about to plant in the earth, never mind how he was managing to dig through frozen ground.

I later cursed myself for not stopping. But truthfully, I had been overtaken as much by fear as by a desire to speak with him again. What was I expecting? That he would have intimate knowledge of my experience? Suppose the healing 'he' had performed was completely unknown to him? Suppose he was just a crazy old man, and not a sage or spiritual being in disguise? These were the doubts running like melt-water beneath the glacier of my frozen views. But it was from these rivulets of uncertainty that I would later reclaim a sense of awe, for I would be faced once more with the fact of not-knowing. But this awareness was embryonic at the time; mainly I felt vexed at my hesitation to stop, and uneasy about the doubts I vaguely knew were responsible. So I privately resolved not to let another opportunity go to waste. The next time I saw him, regardless of the circumstances, I would stop.

About this time, I began to experience a creative renewal. My encounter with the Old Man, and subsequently with Jung, had mingled with my Buddhist studies to form a fertile mulch from which new poems began to shoot – slowly at first, but later in a riot of different blooms and colours. These were combined with poems I had written and published earlier to become the manuscript for my second book, which was published in 2011. In response to one of the complimentary copies which I sent out to friends and associates, I received a remarkable email. A poetry editor who had awarded me first place in an open competition in 2005, and with whom I had stayed in touch, was requesting a meeting over Skype.

"I've read your book and I want you to be my poetry mentor", she said. "I've written and appreciated poetry for years; I've even published poems in journals; but I've never worked with a teacher or tried to assemble a collection. I want you to help me become a better poet, and, maybe, one with a book to her name. And I want to pay you."

I was floored. It was the sort of job I had always wanted – the job I had actually been educated to do. But just beyond my shock and delight, there was something clamouring for my attention; I knew that I couldn't accept monetary payment for this work. My mentor, the poet Fredrick Zydek, had worked tirelessly with me for years on the basis of whatever artistic promise I initially showed, and later, on the strength of the friendship that was forged in the process. There was never any question of *money* being exchanged. We were *poets,* after all – a tribe of seekers, visionaries and outcasts who were in the world but not of it: vagabond-pilgrim-citizens of the realm of song. While my sense of artistic identity had mellowed since my days with Fred, I still knew that I had been the recipient of a rare gift; and just as Fred had been a large-hearted and generous teacher and benefactor, it was time for me to pass the gift on.

"Absolutely not", said Jennifer, the editor; "I won't have you working for me gratis. I need to pay you."

"Not with money", I said. "Poetry's kind of a tribal thing with me; it wouldn't be right."

"Ok", she said, "an exchange of services then. What can I do for you?"

I considered this for a moment. "I'm not sure. What *can* you do for me?"

"Well, I'm also a psychotherapist. I was trained in Gestalt, but for the last twenty years I've had a very strong Jungian orientation…"

I might as well have been surfing the shockwaves of the big bang through the twelfth dimension after those words hit my brain. It was a moment of synchronistic perfection.

Jennifer was already a talented poet and a quick study, and it wasn't long before her work was of such quality that I at times struggled to subdue the competitive impulses it inspired. Conversely, my therapy with Jennifer felt *right* from the very beginning. Despite living on opposite sides of the Atlantic and my initial doubts that therapy via Skype would be a successful venture, I found that it was not vastly different from meeting in person. We quickly developed trust and an authentic rapport, and didn't waste much time before getting to work on the meaty obstructions in my psyche. Much of my work centred on family-of-origin issues, and I learned to come into more intimate contact with my emotions. Most importantly, perhaps, she taught me how to work with my dreams, those nightly missives from the unconscious. Slowly, slowly, I began to understand that health is not the degree to which the light can obliterate the shadows, but the degree to which one's awareness can include both the shadows and the light.

It was also with Jennifer that I first learned about alchemy. With her guidance, I spent nearly two years forging and reinforcing my alchemical container – that heart-space of uncommon sensitivity and strength where difficult emotions can be felt in all their intensity, but are not acted out or visited on others.

"But how does containment lead to transformation?" I asked.

"Got twenty years? I could maybe scratch the surface of that one", said Jennifer. "You see, the container is a kind of crucible, and the alchemy that takes place there really is a transformation of base metal into gold, but of a psycho-spiritual variety."

"But how will I know when I've got the gold?"

"Believe me, you'll know."

So I began the work, and it didn't take long for me to discover that consciously holding the tension of my rage, fear and sadness, was *painful*, and the benefit – the promised shift – seemed always infinitely far into the future. I simply felt no assurance that the outcome would be profound. Thus, my early attempts at holding tension were ambivalent and prematurely terminated. However, I trusted Jennifer, and it was on the strength of her word alone that I persisted. It was not the last time that I would consider faith to be necessary ballast on the voyage of not-knowing.

I seldom thought of the Old Man during this period, though I never failed to look for him when driving on the island. Then, like a remembered dream, the sights, sounds and textures of the incident would return, and I would ponder the same question: had it really happened? It was strange to think that I had memories of the man in two worlds: the world of waking reality that we all inhabit, and a dreamlike world that wasn't a dream. What was the nature of the correspondence between these two realities? Had he (the 'mundane' Old Man) been a conscious interloper in the archetypal realm? Or had my unconscious mind simply borrowed his form in order to heal and teach? It was the prospect of learning the answers to these questions that fuelled my desire to meet him again. But more time would pass, and I would again let the memory slip back into darkness. It would seem a given that I would have processed the content of my experience with the Old Man with Jennifer, but strangely, it never dawned on me to bring it up; another year would pass before I shared with her the story of my archetypal encounter.

About this time, I made my aforementioned trip to Amsterdam. I had long read about the experiences of people who take a psycho-active, plant-based drink called ayahuasca, which delivers to the brain a hefty payload of DMT (dimethyltryptamine) that can result in cathartic, life-changing visions. Ayahuasca has been ritually used for centuries by the indigenous peoples of the Amazon basin, but has recently gained a following among ordinary Brazilians – as well as Americans and Europeans – due to the efforts of the 'ayahuasca churches' which formed in Brazil in the mid-20th century. Naturally, Amsterdam is a European hotspot for people seeking the ayahuasca cure. For reasons that I still can't fully explain, I felt a need to test this therapeutic vehicle for myself. It was an uncharacteristic move for me, as I had no prior history of drug use (beyond the alcoholic escapades of my youth), and the pursuit of an induced psychedelic experience was very much at odds with my Buddhist commitments and practice. But after much study and discernment, ayahuasca had become numinous in my psyche, and the prospect of a chemical *satori* was powerfully compelling.

Though I would have been loath to admit it then, it was another attempt at a magic bullet cure; I was still fishing for a seminal experience that would 'fix' me once and for all. Not only did the visions not manifest (in a room full of people who were clearly having powerful experiences), but the whole endeavour distracted me from the ongoing healing and wisdom available in the vision I *had* received some four years earlier. The Amazon Indians believe that the ayahuasca beverage contains a wise and knowing spirit that gives people exactly what they need. I already had what I needed, but I had forgotten. The Old Man was still waiting in the wings of my psyche for conditions to mature and my understanding to ripen. What my Amsterdam experience *did* do was to expose my tendency toward magical thinking, which would later prove very fruitful for my therapy.

This was a trying period; my work with Jennifer was often difficult, and my experience in Amsterdam (or lack thereof) had left me angry and dejected. Worse still, my creative outpouring seemed to have reached a caesura, and for months my attempts at writing poetry languished in the doldrums. The Old Man was so distant a memory as to be non-existent, and when I did remember, I was involved in a wrong-headed attempt to discern a mortal man's role in my inner experience. I was at a high and narrow place, and a step in any direction was a step too far. There was nothing left for me to fall back on. I had no more resources or will with which to distract myself from the important if discomforting work at hand: mastering the use of the alchemical container.

It's difficult to put into words just how angst-inducing and scratch-my-way-out-of-my-skin uncomfortable this process was. As before, the act of holding the tension of my faulty thinking and difficult emotions felt interminable, except for death or madness. But slowly, imperceptibly even, I developed stamina, and was able to hold my feelings for longer and longer periods. I look back on these months like it was a trip to the realm of the dead; all of my calculation and external focus had been exhausted, and I gave almost all my time to Buddhist meditation, reading, and working with the episodes of my life that allowed me to practice containment. And, critically, I literally gave up hope that the discomfort would ever end. It felt very much like a kind of dying; the constant and profound sadness I experienced was of a quality that I have never known before or since. As I said to Jennifer, it wasn't just *my* sadness; I felt like I was carrying and bearing witness to the sadness of the whole world.

*

Then one day, it happened. I don't even remember the catalysing event (such trifles I was working with!), but something occurred that gave me the opportunity to practise. By this time, I had developed strength enough that I could hold the tension of my feelings while doing something else, remaining more or less mindful of both the practice and the task before me. So there I was, washing the dishes and minding my mind when, suddenly, the tension I was holding spontaneously and abruptly released. Immediately, I was flooded with a joy that I had not felt since being healed by the Old Man.

I started to laugh. Jennifer was right in claiming to need at least twenty years to explain it; how can one fully explain what happens in that instant when the chemical spark leaps the synapse? The feeling was like being swept up in a huge wave of relief – but not a backward-looking relief at the tension finally easing, or at being released from pain. It was relief at being able to survey the vista that now unfurled itself before my mind's eye. There was such *light* on the other side of containment: a light that was soft and suffusing, but also brighter than the flashpoint of creation. It held and embraced me, just as I was, but also burned away the dross of my psyche so that my Shadow could be seen and cognised. I was joyful, euphoric even, but in a quieter, less dramatic way than in the wake of my encounter with the Old Man. *Relief* is the word I keep coming back to, for I now knew that the light was there; I had 'seen' it for myself, and that seeing could never be undone. Though it would necessarily recede from my consciousness (who among us can live constantly in such light?), I knew by which means it was manifest. Holding the tension of my Shadow material was the high and demanding art necessary to alchemise base metals into gold.

I'm sure the reader has by now seen a connection that would take me many more months to see: that my experience with the Old Man was a foreshadowing of this process. He had modelled and embodied the alchemical container for me; his willingness to take into himself and hold my Shadow material, my base metal, is precisely what allowed him to show me the substance of my true nature. One must enter the crucible to be transformed – and be willing to suffer the discomfort and, yes, pain, of transformation. The painful ordeal that he willingly suffered on my behalf pointed toward the bravery that this work requires, for transformation necessarily entails the letting go of old patterns of thinking and being in the world. It can feel like death, and probably always carries with it a savour of the grave no matter how long one has practised. Each time I enter the alchemical container, it is an act of faith; I can never be certain of the outcome, despite having gone through it a great many times. Naturally, it has grown easier with repetition, but there is always in the background the fear that, *this* time, the process will overwhelm me – or that I will wait in vain for the gold. In the intensity of the container, there is no room for pride, for practice is always a leap into the unknown.

There was another, unforeseen benefit of experiencing my first alchemical work: the nature and identity of the Old Man no longer troubled me. I had experienced exactly what I had experienced: one man, two worlds. Was it the same man in both? Did I encounter an archetypal projection from my unconscious in a deep state of reverie? Or was he truly a Bodhisattva, or as Jennifer said, an angel? Did it really matter? And if I could know the answers to these questions, would I really want to?

Not very long prior to this writing, I was driving out on the island on some errand or other. I was not on the job, and drove unhurriedly past the farms and fields and woods of String Valley Road. Suddenly, there he was, walking down the shoulder of the road, his blue robe wrapping him like a flame. I slowed down a little, wondering at first if it was really him. Then I saw the piece of white plastic around his head, holding his long hair back from his face in the gusts of wind that rolled in from the coast. I smiled as I discreetly placed my hands together and gave a small bow – whether to a man or spiritual being, I had no idea.

And no way of knowing. My mind on fire with gratitude and with awe, I drove past without stopping.

The Contributors

Manu Bazzano is a writer, psychotherapist and supervisor in private practice, primary tutor at Metanoia Institute, visiting lecturer at Roehampton University and various other schools and colleges. He facilitates workshops and seminars internationally. Among his books are: *Buddha is Dead; Spectre of the Stranger; After Mindfulness.* Forthcoming titles by Manu include *Therapy and the Counter-tradition: the Edge of Philosophy*, co-edited with Julie Webb, and *Zen and Therapy*, both published by Routledge. **www.manubazzano.com**

Caroline Brazier is course leader of the Tariki Training Programme and author of six books on Buddhism and psychotherapy. **www.tarikitrust.org**

Alex Buchan has studied under various Buddhist meditation masters in the Theravada, Zen and Tibetan traditions and undertook an MA in Buddhist Studies under Peter Harvey. Having previously worked as a nurse therapist in an NHS psychotherapy day centre, he later undertook a Buddhist informed training in counselling at the Amida Trust.

Paul Christelis is a psychotherapist, writer and mindfulness teacher. He is co-director of School of Moments, an organisation dedicated to promoting presence and deepening resilience at work, at home and in play. **www.schoolofmoments.com**

Ian Finlay has been a student of comparative religion for nearly 50 years, with particular emphasis on Buddhism, although he is also a Quaker and interested in non-dualism. He feels passionately about wildlife, conservation and the rights of tribal peoples. He lives near Aberystwyth in Wales where he manages his own woodland which is sometimes used for ecotherapy.

Mia Livingston is a Zen Buddhist writer. Having lived in three different continents and in a monastery, she writes about how Zen practice applies to relationships and social issues. Her work has featured in *The Guardian*, on the BBC and on TEDx. She has worked as editor for the Buddhist Society's quarterly journal, and is training in psychotherapy. **www.mialivingston.com**

Dr Rosemary Lodge is a counselling psychologist and senior lecturer at Regent's University London. Her therapeutic orientation is existential/person-centred and she has a special interest in children and families, gender, and the emotional or unspoken aspects of the therapeutic relationship. She also has a private practice and has experience of working with children and adolescents in schools.

Margaret Meyer is an integrative counsellor and bibliotherapist, working in private practice and within the prison service. Her book on therapeutic metaphor is under contract with Crown House publishers.
www.margaretmeyer-therapy.co.uk

Owen Okie, MSc. Herbal Medicine, is a herbalist, HeartMath Provider and counsellor in training with a passion for nature, music, science, spirituality, healing and transformation. He co-founded EarthMind Fellowship, CIC, a social enterprise dedicated to bringing people into deep contact with nature and running nature-based programs for exploration, healing and growth.
www.integralherbalism.wordpress.com ~ www.earthmindfellowship.org

Andy Paice lived and practised as a monastic in the Kagyu tradition of Tibetan Buddhism at Kundrol Ling monastery in France from 1998-2007 where he accomplished a traditional three-year group retreat. He then returned to the lay life in London and pursues interests in Western psychotherapy, group dynamics and social activism. He is a coach, facilitator, mindfulness trainer, community builder and advocate for a participatory society. **www.andypaice.net**

Jason Ranek is a poet, essayist and freelance journalist living in Norway. His latest book, *The Crossing*, is available at Amazon.com.

The Editors

Bob Chisholm is a psychotherapist and counsellor in Canterbury, UK who uses ideas from Buddhist psychology in his approach to psychotherapy.

He writes a regular blog, which can be found at:

bobchisholmcounselling.com

Jeff Harrison is a psychotherapist, supervisor, trainer and writer. He manages the counselling service at a college in central London.

He has a PhD comparing Buddhist psychology with Western models.

About the Publisher

Triarchy Press is an independent publisher of interesting, original and alternative thinking (altThink) about:

- organisations and government, financial and social systems - and how to make them work better
- human beings and the ways in which they participate in the world – moving, walking, thinking, dreaming, suffering and loving.

Other titles of possible interest include:

Windows Kiss the Shadows of the Passing Thirty Million – Robert Golden
A narrative poem about exile, human displacement and migration.

Silent Music – Julian Wolfreys
A novel that explores through its narrative and the central analogy between love and music, ideas of loss, grief and absence at the intersection of memory studies, psychoanalysis, philosophy, historiography, rhetoric and poststructuralism.

Nothing Special: Experiencing Fear and Vulnerability in Daily Life
– Mary Booker
A collection of poetry, prose, photographs and personal experience, written by a noted dramatherapist on the experience of vulnerability.

Nine Ways of Seeing a Body – Sandra Reeve
Nine different approaches to the human body as seen in movement, performance and psychotherapy.

Growing Wings on the Way: Systems Thinking for Messy Situations
– Rosalind Armson
A practical guide to using Systems Thinking to think your way through the most intractable of personal, social or organisational problem.

www.triarchypress.net

Lightning Source UK Ltd.
Milton Keynes UK
UKOW06f1233141016

285227UK00007B/40/P

9 781909 470910